Ode to Jol

Ode to Jol

Alasdair Gold

SPORTS
BOOKS

Published in Great Britain by
SportsBooks Limited
PO Box 422
Cheltenham
GL50 2YN
Tel: 01242 256755
Fax: 01242 254694
email: info@sportsbooks.ltd.uk
www.sportsbooks.ltd.uk

© Alasdair Gold 2006
First Published September 2006

Front cover designed by Kath Northam.
Front cover photograph: Actionimages.
Back cover and other photographs: Empics.

A catalogue record for this book is available from
the British Library.

ISBN 1 899807 43 8

Printed by Cromwell Press

To Carly, Ryan, Amy and Lana for being there in the real world that exists outside White Hart Lane, constantly ready to drag me back from the brink.

Contents

Acknowledgements

THERE ARE SO many people to thank for their help in the season-long journey that is this book.

First up I have to thank my wife Carly and our children Ryan, Amy and Lana. I consider myself extremely fortunate that rather than feeling the need to attack me with kitchen implements every time I switched on the television, radio or internet for the latest Spurs news, I got only encouragement. Thanks for making the defeats that bit easier to take and suffering my Spurs-induced moods.

Next on the gratitude trail are my parents, June and Sidney, for always drumming it into me to make sure I do the things in life I want to do rather than settle for the dross that others think I should do.

Cheers to everyone at Spurscommunity who introduced me to the true scale of Spurs supporting across the globe.

Thanks to Rob for appointing me the site's editor despite having only a handful of articles to my name. I hope I continue to grow as the site does and we enjoy the coming seasons together as much as we have this one.

Thanks to all the other football websites including Squarefootball, COYS, Fromthelane, Spursodyssey and Football Fanzone, all of which have posted my work and hopefully enjoyed it. I've made a lot of friends and you've all helped me along the way.

Further gratitude to Toby Allanson who joins me every day in my day job. It is always helpful to hear his weekly views on my opinions, whether they include a laugh, nod, sigh or a stern rebuke. I often need to be reminded to keep my optimism in check, even if he fails the majority of the time.

Thanks to Richard Bloss for always listening to my constant drivel and donating his ideas for the look of the book. Long may our working relationship continue.

There's definitely a load more people out there who have helped me on my way and don't be insulted if I've failed to mention you here. You're all as important to this book as I am and just because my memory failed me today doesn't detract from my gratitude.

Introduction

A Womb with a View

MY PARENTS LIVED in Loughton at the end of the free and hairy seventies. Even my father, not an avid follower of fashion, had sideburns that could tickle the faces of passing pedestrians. He had always supported Tottenham Hotspur because he came from Golders Green. He was a London boy.

The players at the time reflected the football being played. The long locks of Villa and Chivers encapsulated the flair and flamboyance of the Spurs attacking style. The White Hart Lane faithful seem to have always appreciated their long-haired maestros whatever the decade.

Later idols like Hoddle, Waddle and Ginola all had hair that belonged to an era long gone, but they still somehow managed to glide effortlessly with the ball past stunned opponents, perhaps leaving them choking on split ends and the faint tune of *Diamond Lights* burning in their ears.

Anyway, back to me. According to my mother, I was not a particularly active baby to carry to term. That is, except for an hour or so every Saturday night, when I used to kick the hell out of my poor mother's innards.

If my parents are to be believed, then as soon as the famed *Match of the Day* theme music would kick off on the BBC, I would go crazy. In a taster of the man to come, those little legs would hit every beat and simulate each volley, flick and diving header. I'm not sure if there's ever been a recorded case of pre-natal keepy-uppy, but I'd like to put my name forward.

It was definitely a dose of the future and for the next 26 years, football dominated my life. Nothing outside the game, and I mean nothing, could quite replicate the feeling of Gazza's free kick against the Gooners in the FA Cup semi-final or Jürgen Klinsmann's flying arrival at N17.

When I was ten years old, playing in my garden, pretending to be Gary Lineker, knocking the ball past my stranded father, mother, sister, even the dog on occasions, it was everything. Each time I closed my eyes, I was there on the famous gleaming, green pitch with 36,000 fans screaming in celebration around me. Sad as it may be, sixteen years later, sitting at my desk, the same thing happens every so often when those eyelids shut.

We Spurs fans are a rare breed, always looking on the bright side of the Lane whatever the weather a few blocks away. Only a Lilywhite could, despite years of inconsistency and a slightly dusty trophy cabinet, dream every summer of an endless conveyor belt full of Galacticos heading into Tottenham.

There's no doubting that things have gone rather badly in recent years down at White Hart Lane and the grand old cockerel has not worn its smile in a long time. Spurs have changed managers with such frequency that the reign of Bill Nicholson and his glory glory days almost seem the stuff of legend and myth.

For younger fans, there's been precious little to back up the claims of our fathers and grandfathers that Spurs were once the team that others aspired to copy as we set record after record. Everything seemed to be pointing towards a continued slide into mediocrity when something fantastic happened. The old club began to shake off the cobwebs and wake up again.

A Womb with a View

White Hart Lane began to resemble a train station platform as more and more fresh faces appeared each day and carriage-loads of ageing, overpaid pros were whisked off to smaller clubs around the country. Talented youngsters with suitcases full of potential arrived outside the club's doors with big smiles on their faces and dreams of the Premiership.

This last campaign saw heroes born and villains made. There were cheers, boos and laughs as entertainment of some sort was brought to the crowds. Whether it was from the players or the staff, there was always some act of tragedy, comedy or drama to witness in the theatre of the Lane.

There were highs and lows every single week of the season with shocks, spills and stunning moments in abundance. This is the story of the season when one man, with the glint of Sir Bill in his eye, stamped his mark on the club and it became fun to be a Spurs supporter again…

Chapter One

Pre-season
It Started with a Twist

Saturday June 4th 2005

IT SEEMS LIKE only yesterday I was screaming at anyone who would listen that I had been stabbed in the back by Jacques Santini, now the man who headed up the Dream Team has plunged another knife into the wound.

I guess the fact that we made Frank Arnesen a deity at the Lane has made his fall from grace all the more spectacular and painful. Santini got stick early on from fans and media alike and although it was a shock when he walked, there was a man ready to step into his shoes. But Frank was the hero, the one who was leading the revolution and pulling the strings.

Daniel Levy said that the beauty of the European management system was that if the head coach left then the impact was lessened and some degree of continuity was kept behind the scenes. What his plan didn't take into account was that some invading Russian devil could cut the head off the snake. What happens when the man in charge of the whole system walks?

I don't know what sickens me more. That Chelsea can stride around the Premiership, flouting rules as they wish and plucking anyone they care for from the world's top teams without fear of consequences. Or that Frank Arnesen, who was meant to be the saviour, could walk out after only one season, eyes glistening with dollar signs.

Only a month ago, he was turning down a switch to Valencia as he was very happy with life in North London. Yet despite calling for Jol to disregard the lure of Ajax, and Defoe, King and Robinson to ignore lucrative moves because something big was happening at White Hart Lane, the Dane decided hypocrisy was the best dish on the menu.

This lump in the back of my throat is really getting on my nerves. It sounds stupid to say but it's not far off the one I had when 'Sir' Bill died last year. Whenever managers have left Tottenham in recent years, it's often been with a P45 flapping in their hands. To lose Arnesen to another club is a far more foreign concept and it hurts like hell. I guess now I know how Southampton feel.

Nothing seems to happen at White Hart Lane without a circus and the double act of mayhem and chaos close behind. It may put us on the back pages, but we ultimately end up looking like plonkers. I do feel for Daniel Levy because he seems to be trying his hardest to drag the club out of obscurity but people just keep throwing spanners in the works.

With the latest chapter, it turns out that those kind folks at Chelsea sent a letter asking Levy if they could speak to Frank Arnesen about turning to the dark side. What they failed to mention to the diminutive chairman was that they had also sent a copy of the letter to our Sporting Director just to make sure he was aware of the offer. An illegal approach without any permission, surely?

Trying to put aside the burning feeling in my chest for Frank's hypocritical show of coldness I can only feel that Chelski decided to stick a money-covered bomb into White Hart Lane purely because they saw us as a long-term threat. I'm very surprised that Jose Mourinho feels he needs a Sporting Director or that the club feels it needs cheap youth players when they are buying the world's best 22-to-24-year-olds.

It smacks of jealousy and fear and is surely a guffaw in the face of the FA who decided to laughably confiscate the Russian club's spare change this week. Managers, chief executives, players and now sporting directors; if Chelsea want them, they just steamroll in and take them regardless of contracts. Who's going to stop them?

So where does this truly leave the club? On the plus side, Defoe has signed a new deal, Routledge has already signed the pre-contract agreement and John McDermott has just been appointed as Academy Manager, so the future of the club in that respect is sorted. On the negative side, Robinson was due to sign a new deal in a matter of days: will he now? King and Jol were also due new deals: where do they stand?

What happens with Arnesen? He's suspended and will presumably never work for Spurs again. He's shown his loyalty lies with a bank note. This will drag on for some time and I'm only hoping it won't muck up our transfer plans or put people off coming to North London. I'd personally like to see Chelsea banned from making approaches for playing or management staff for the season or if we do lose Arnesen to them then the compensation or damages should be extremely significant. Enough to bring in someone special to lift the gloom – hello Mr Wright-Phillips.

The burning question now is do we stick with the continental system or will Jol be given the key to the Lane? As much as I liked the new set-up, will we find a better Sporting Director out there? I know Trapattoni is free now but would the ageing Italian, having just won the Portuguese title with Benfica, take on that role? Or if he is still homesick then how about the unemployed Louis Van Gaal? Would it be worth bringing in a new guy though, who may not agree with all the young English talents we have brought in?

Could the Jolly Orange Giant not become our Alex Ferguson with a bumper new contract? Let him bring in another assistant from Holland to ease the burden a little and run the club. As my rage begins to simmer a little, I'm beginning to look towards the latter idea. Jol wants to be the new Bill Nicholson so why not let him?

It hurts like a slap in the face with a spiked glove but tomorrow truly is another day and brings with it the promise of European football in the Uefa Fair Play draw. As last season's highest placed fair side, we have a chance to sneak into the Uefa Cup, because we simply didn't put enough tackles in. It's hardly the most glamorous route into Europe, but I'm not too big to beg or clutch blindly at straws. With the plucking of a certain ball from a bag, a whole host of fresh talented faces could be knocking on the door at White Hart Lane.

The blueprints have already been laid on the table for the revival of Tottenham Hotspur. The youngsters who will be legends of the future are already in place and Jol knows who he still needs to take the team to the next level. The King is dead, I say long live the King.

Sunday June 5th 2005

Uefa Fair Play Draw at the City of Manchester Stadium

A DANISH CLUB – as yet unknown as their season has not finished – and German side Mainz were chosen to take part. There were reports that the Tottenham ball was picked first but officials merely laughed and chucked it into a nearby dustbin.

Sunday July 8th 2005

I'VE JUST SPENT the last two weeks supposedly taking a break, away from unfair play draws, in a sleepy village 10 minutes from the Mediterranean coast. While others were enjoying the spectacular views or lying burning on the beach, yours truly was berating a little old Spanish woman for failing to stock English newspapers.

With sweat dripping down my reddening face, I pleaded with the wrinkly prune to tell me where I could buy a decent tabloid just to scan the back pages. As I waved euros in front of her cackling face, she just blanked me completely and served another customer. Didn't she understand that five days of the holiday had passed and I knew nothing about the goings on at White Hart Lane?

It wasn't long until I cracked and shouted something about Spanish shops being stuck in the Dark Ages and that I needed some bloody gossip about Tottenham Hotspur. She stopped giggling and looked me straight in the eyes. She came around the counter and put her hand on my shoulder before pulling a scrap of paper from a shelf.

In broken English she read: "For news on Tottingham Hotspur, go to big supermarket in next town of Denia. Papers are very expensive but you will pay, no?" She looked up. I nodded and she pushed me gently through the door into the burning daylight. I realised then that I wasn't the first desperate holidaying Yiddo to walk through that door and I certainly wouldn't be the last.

We definitely are a rare breed. I don't know of any other type of fan who devours transfer gossip so readily. Who cares if a rumour has been texted to a journalist by an eight-year-old girl? As long as they call her a source close to Christian Vieri or an insider at White Hart Lane, it'll grab my attention and have me salivating messily about the future.

It Started with a Twist

Most clubs would be delighted with five players signed in the summer, but something tells me that after last season's record haul of imports that just won't do. I do rate Routledge very highly having caught a lot of Palace games last season. I genuinely believe that by next July the skilful youngster will be one of the big players at the Lane and perhaps another Lion.

It surprises me when people think we've aimed low by going for the 20-year-old England U21 winger. Bizarrely, the fact that he's proven in the Premiership counts against him with preference given to excitingly named foreigners from lightweight leagues that most fans have only read about on a website. Perhaps that's when the crazy links with global superstars begin to cloud our judgement a little. I've been guilty of it myself.

I haven't seen as much of pint-sized Aaron Lennon but I assume he'll initially struggle to make the striker-adorned bench and we'll see more of him as the inevitable injuries kick in. I know far more about Tom Huddlestone and I feel this season he'll fit in wherever a space appears, be it in defence or midfield. Next season he'll have to choose what he wants to be. Just ask Gary Doherty where being versatile gets you.

Paul Stalteri and Teemu Tainio add to the new blend with some much needed experience. The former has won the league and cup double in Germany while the latter has bagfuls of European experience and a lot of talent to utilise. To top it all he's an avid Spurs fan like us. Not just a new recruit saying "I used to like Jürgen Klinsmann" but a fully-fledged fan since childhood.

On Wednesday it was revealed that Frank "I like da rouble" Arnesen is staying with us until September 1st. I'm actually split on the club's decision. I like the fact that he can't help Chelski buy anyone this window and, as we did with him and Pleat, there could be a handing over period between him and his successor.

The downside depends on whether he'll be allowed to sign players for Spurs during the next two months. If he is then something I heard another fan say must surely come to the fore. When he's selling the club to a player, what's to stop them saying: "If it's so great, why are you leaving?" It doesn't fill me with confidence.

Also, if he does come across another Reto Ziegler, what's to stop him taking a sneaky peek from side to side, scribbling his name down in his little blue book, and then reporting back with: "No, sorry Danny boy, nothing today." But of course, I'm sure he'd never betray us. Wow, I really used to think that.

Who knows what's on the horizon. We've been linked with the sublime (Vieri, Saviola and D'Alessandro) to the ridiculous (Harewood, Lua Lua and Crouch). Speculated targets have come and gone in the shape of Downing, Parker, Figo and Vieri. One thing's looking increasingly likely in that the next player we bring in is probably going to be someone we hadn't even thought of.

The excitement is palpable as tomorrow brings with it our first pre-season friendly in the form of traditional opponents Stevenage Borough. Our reserve affiliation with their ground usually ensures we put out a strong side. Jol has already said we'll probably see Routledge, Tainio and Huddlestone and possibly Lennon. Stalteri is injured as is England's Number One.

Pretty much all the big names will get some time on the pitch and it'll hopefully be a taster of what's to come. Any bets on Routledge's first goal with a magnificent solo effort? It'll be interesting to see where Tainio is deployed across the midfield and whether Andy Reid and Mido, if he's fit, have shed some major poundage under club orders. Then next weekend will see us take part in the Peace Cup with the majority, if not all the games, being shown on Eurosport, starting with our opener against Boca Juniors.

The days are flying by and August 13th and Fratton Park are edging closer. The Jolly Giant is assembling his forces and training them hard for the ten-month campaign ahead.

There's no doubting that this season should see one of the youngest, hungriest teams in Tottenham history with quality teeming throughout the squad, not just on the team sheet. Can you hear that? That sound in the distance? I do believe it's a cockerel starting to crow again.

Friday July 22nd 2005

WHAT A DIFFERENCE a year makes. As July drew to a close last year the club was in a hazy world of the unknown. There were changes at the top, the squad was transformed, even the Jammy Dodgers in the players' canteen were swapped for Custard Creams.

The confusion was not helped in any way by David "I get paid by Portsmouth to cuddle Laurent Robert" Pleat's insistence on booking us up for a squad-draining 12 friendlies against the might of Hull, Trollhattans, Sheffield United and Cagliari. The new set-up didn't stand a chance of seeing the first eleven together.

Matches came thick and fast and reserves, donkeys and kids were all mixed in with the tired stars. I'm sure during one match we had a central defensive pairing of Gary Doherty and Macaulay Culkin. No doubt Jacko was in the stands, Johnnie that is. The predictable happened and we played extremely poorly and disjointedly, winning a mere two out of the 12 with historic victories against Stevenage and Nottingham Forest.

As a little aside, I was told recently by a friend who

looks after the players, that, during training matches, Inspector Santini used to blow a whistle every time a left or right-back crossed the halfway line. The other eleven were then awarded a free kick. It used to irritate the hell out of everyone but in a way probably contributed to the group bonding against the Frenchman. The ultra defensive full-backs would become a feature of Jacques' reign.

So 12 months on and I doubt you could find a much different pre-season. Rather than 12 matches, we have only seven including a lucrative Asian tournament pitting us against some top footballing teams. What better experience to give our starlets than contests against the dribbling South Americans, the Spaniards with their technique and passing, the emerging South Africans and finally a French side in Lyon that surprised everyone in the Champions League last season?

Rather than trotting out against lower league English opposition, the players are getting a sample of every possible style of opponent they can face. Not only that but a nice pot of Korean gold sits at the end of the rainbow if we can just prod Gerard Houllier's frog eyes away from it.

We are unbeaten so far in our travels which is a nice alternative to last year's losses to Scottish sides and Sheffield United. However, as I said then, the scoreline, while it does boost morale, is secondary to fitness building, team bonding and giving Martin Jol a chance to assess the new players and how others have developed.

The new players on show so far have impressed. The big Dutchman has given Teemu Tainio a lot of time on the pitch. Having initially heard he was a defensive midfielder, it would seem that the Finn is more a box to box player and needs the pre-season to build up the necessary stamina.

His flicks and passes to the strikers and wingers could be a vital addition to the team in an area where we have been lacking. His runs into the box indicate that a central midfielder may actually pick up some goals in the coming season. Jol has taken time out to praise him and I think that the Spurs-supporting maestro could surprise the Premiership this season.

I'm not going to say too much about Wayne Routledge as without harping on I see him becoming the right-sided Ginola of our time. We've seen flashes of his ability in the Peace Cup and against Stevenage. His feet are quicker than a Darren Day engagement and, as his fitness builds, that long-needed pace and magic will provide us with a potent weapon against teams we normally struggle to break down. I wouldn't be shocked if Sven finds himself with a similar selection headache with Wayne as he did with Defoe before Euro 2004.

Aaron Lennon and Tom Huddlestone have been used sparingly but have looked like raw talents ready for the Giant to mould. Lennon has pace but needs to work on his control and end product while Huddlestone played almost every minute of England's involvement in the U20 Toulon Tournament and is probably being given a break.

Jol has preferred Gardner and Davenport since King and Dawson's respective cramp and nose-breaking exploits, but then Bunjevcevic and Richards played a lot of friendlies last summer. Davenport has looked shaky in moments but then playing for Southampton will do that to you. With Stalteri still to make his entrance, the squad is undoubtedly looking a lot stronger than it has done for years.

In the last weeks, there have been rumours of a Beast around White Hart Lane. As monster hunters and tourists flocked to North London to snap the spectacle, it was revealed that the beast was in fact the Brazilian Julio Baptista, a 7ft 8ins, 34-stone, midfielder turned striker playing in Spain.

My heart tells me that Baptista would consider a move to Tottenham with reports of him following the Lilywhites as a youngster. However, my brain tells me it's the most unlikely negotiation since Neville Chamberlain asked Adolf Hitler if he fancied dropping the whole war thing and coming over for tea instead.

That's not to say it'll never happen; Klinsmann and Rebrov are examples that it can, but the weight of logic says it won't. The player himself wants to gain dual Spanish nationality in order to make life easier for himself and has admitted in the past that a move to Barcelona would be a dream.

If he were to come to England, I'm afraid the lure of a fading team in the Champions League appeals to players more than joining a team on the rise. Money and being in the media spotlight will always beat a challenge and becoming a legend today.

With the bid perhaps more a statement of intent by Daniel Levy, I think there will be at least one more signing before the season begins with an attacking midfielder still high on the agenda. A number of players seem to still be clinging onto the pegs in the changing rooms at Spurs Lodge and they will have to be yanked out if we are to trim the weak from our 67-strong squad.

As usual, the excitement is growing steadily as the new season slinks ever closer. I'll even get up early on Sunday to catch our Peace Cup final against Lyon. I think Mavis the cleaner had better start dusting the trophy shelves at the Lane. I've got a feeling this Korean trinket won't be the only piece of silverware to grace the cabinet this campaign.

Sunday July 24th 2005

Peace Cup Final
Tottenham Hotspur 3 Lyon 1
Attendance – 48,734
Spurs goalscorers: Keane 2, Kelly

Friday August 5th 2005

THERE'S A CRACKLING in the air around White Hart Lane. The place is quite literally buzzing according to passers-by. There were even reports this week that Martin Jol had been spotted standing on top of the golden cockerel booming a mighty laugh across North London.

At the same time, Arsène Whinger was late for a press conference after he was found by press officers hiding in a cupboard in the canteen. He was crouching in a corner in a puddle of greenish liquid, mumbling: "Make 'im stop. Make 'im stop."

There is definitely something brewing in N17. Cornflakes are being spilt everywhere with people reading their morning papers in shock as yet another journalist or manager tips the current Spurs squad for big things. The really frightening thing is that they were doing this in the days and weeks before we signed one of the biggest footballing names of the modern era.

The capture of the bespectacled Edgar Davids cannot be underestimated in any form. Jürgen Klinsmann came to the Lane when he was 30 and then returned when he was 33. Age was hardly a factor then as he first took us up a level in the eyes of the footballing world or when he returned on a white horse to save us from sinking back down.

At 32, his Dutch successor is acknowledged as one of the fittest players on the global stage. Much has been made of his lack of games last season for Inter but I think it's a perfect gift to Tottenham. The freshness of his body will mean we are pretty much being handed for nothing the same player who reinvigorated Barcelona a year ago.

Some prefer to credit that Spanish revival to the Brazilian Ronaldinho but the majority of people in the game beg to differ. Barcelona's sports secretary Aitor "Txiki" Begiristain said after the turnaround: "The team is very young and isn't tired when it gets to the second half of games. Rijkaard came up with a tactical system and requested one player, Davids, the type of player Barcelona didn't have and needed."

Sound familiar? A young team with that missing piece being slotted into the jigsaw. A giant rising from its slumber. With Real Madrid looking over their shoulders at the rapidly climbing Catalans with a snorting Pitbull leading them on, defender Michel Salgado couldn't have put it any clearer, saying: "Davids is proving more important that Ronaldinho."

It's all about taking the team up to the next level. If having the earnest Michael Brown in your midfield is like putting an average but reliable Ford engine in your car, then having the snarling Davids dropped in there brings more horsepower than a Ferrari–Chevrolet love child. Is anyone else as excited about seeing him lock horns with Keane, Gerrard and Makelele as I am?

When in our generation have we had a midfielder who has the ability rather than merely the potential to dump on the best from a great height? Out of interest, am I the only person who keeps seeing flashes of all his many ultra-cool Nike adverts in their mind and thinks, "Bloody hell, he's going to pull on a Spurs shirt tomorrow"? Those Everton fans must be similarly thrilled about snapping up world icon Phil Neville.

It Started with a Twist

I must apologise if the optimism and excitement levels are approaching boiling point, but it's not often this happens. Since the club decided to prematurely announce the signing after a psychic tapped into Edgar's thoughts, I have been living in a state of delirium.

There we were with a handful of predicted signings, pretty much all signalled from afar in the press, and a successful and encouraging Peace Cup win. Then Levy goes and spoils it all by saying something stupid like "I got Davids".

Can you imagine the effect our new number five's experience and talent will have on youngsters like Routledge, Carrick, Reid, Ziegler, Lennon and Defoe? As Jol said, he brings with him the aura of a winner. In Tom Huddlestone, the Dutchman also has the chance to bring forth his footballing offspring ready to take on his mantle, when the dreadlocks have become grey and the glasses horn-rimmed.

There is a chance that my senses may go into meltdown next Saturday morning as my postponed freebie tour of White Hart Lane is due to take place on the very day we begin our assault on the Premiership. Don't judge me too harshly when you read reports in the Sunday papers of a man breaking into all the club's rooms, yelling in vain at shocked employees: "Martin, I love you!" So what if the big man happens to be on the south coast that day. Don't bore me with the facts, they just slow me down.

This season my voice will truly never have been louder, more passionate or more supportive. I will witness this team being born on the pitch, in the stands, in the pubs, in my living room, on my radio and on my computer.

As fans we must be united in unwavering support for our mighty Jolly General, his bespectacled right-hand man and those young talented troops. In years to come, we'll be able to tell our grandchildren that this was the season when that ole Spurs magic made its spectacular return.

Thursday August 11th 2005

SOME CONVERSATIONS AND meetings that may have taken place in and around White Hart Lane over the summer months...

A figure is sprinting through Waltham Forest

ARSÈNE WENGER RUNS through the forest, his face smeared with blood and sweat. His skin is drained of colour and he's breathing heavily. As the emaciated Frenchman scurries between the trees, he constantly looks back into the dense forest, scanning the treetops with his beady eyes.

With his skinny legs burning from fear and pain, he dives behind a large log and lies behind it, head close to the ground. His whole body is streaked in mud from his desperate run. Blood oozes from a shoulder wound. He screams into the dense woodland.

AW: Who the hell are you?

From the trees comes a rasping noise which becomes clearer and slowly Wenger realises it is his own words being repeated. He peeks over the log and sees something shimmering in the air six feet away.

Suddenly, the shape drops its cloak of invisibility and the dreadlocked form of Edgar Davids stands before the trembling Frenchman. The goggled hunter lets out a mighty bellowing roar that echoes around the trees, sending birds and bats flying from their branches. Wenger cowers.

AW: Please don't hurt me.

The muscular midfielder grabs him by the throat and hoists him up into the air. He takes off his goggles with his other hand to reveal terrifying yellow eyes. A greenish puddle forms below the Frenchman. Davids looks down at it and then back, deep into Wenger's eyes.

ED: Go back and tell them about me. Their time has come.

He releases his grip and the skinny manager falls to the ground, struggling to breathe. He splutters for a moment and then looks up. He is alone.

Teemu Tainio and Paul Stalteri are walking around the offices of White Hart Lane

TT: What's in this one?

He opens a door and finds Martin Jol holding a puffy-faced Frank Arnesen in a headlock. He is repeatedly punching him.

MJ: That's from Ledley. This one's from Jermain. That's from Mido... .

He notices the two new signings.

MJ: Is it September 1st already?

Paul shakes his head. Martin gives a toothy grin.

MJ: Good. We've got a big squad to get through.

He goes back to Frank's 'gardening leave' as the new boys close the door.

The players are entering the White Hart Lane car park for the Porto friendly

THERE IS A long procession of expensive cars waiting to be let into the main car park of the stadium. Jermain Defoe, Ledley King and Michael Carrick all pull their sports cars and jeeps past the security guard.

As the last car goes in, the guard notices a small donkey behind it, wandering up the road towards the entrance. Sitting astride it is Pedro Mendes. He rides round the corner and up to the guard.

Guard: Sorry, Pedro. There's no room at the Lane.

PM: But… but

Guard: Sorry mate, we're all midfieldered out.

Pedro turns his donkey around and trots sadly off. As he makes his way down the High Street, he hears the booming chant of "Edgar, Edgar" coming from the White Hart Lane faithful. He stops.

PM: No more, donkey. This is not fair. Father, have you forsaken me?

He looks to the sky but the "Edgar" chant only grows louder. He steps from his animal and raises his hands to the sky. The clouds darken and the winds rise. Lightning begins to streak across the heavens.

PM: I've done nothing wrong yet they chant the name of false prophets. Why, father, why?

A massive bolt of lightning suddenly smashes down from the sky and stops inches from the golden cockerel sitting on top of the stadium. There is a collective gasp from the 36,000-strong crowd as they see it hovering there.

PM: No! Not here. There!

With a wave of his hands the bolt flies across North London, smashing into a crane on a building site. The crane topples into another and then another, creating a domino effect that within seconds brings the shell of the Emirates Stadium crashing to the ground.

The dark clouds part and Pedro gets back on his donkey and heads off down the road. Slowly the strains of "Pedro, Pedro" grow from behind him. He smiles to himself and continues on his journey.

The Inter Milan players are training on the San Siro pitch the night before a friendly

THEY ARE DISTURBED by a commotion in the tunnel. Two men have broken free of security guards' clutches and are running towards the pitch. They are Johnnie Jackson and Goran Bunjevcevic.

JJ: All right Bunje mate, we've made it. What a deal eh? A year in the wilderness and now this.

GB: I know, my friend. I couldn't believe my ears when Mr Levy said we were part of the transfer for Davids.

Johnnie steals the ball off a stunned Adriano and knocks it to his mate.

JJ: Buongiorno boys. You've got yourselves one hell of a pair here. Come on Goran, let's show 'em what we're made of. Wait... Wait!

The two players are dragged off the pitch by Italian policemen who beat them senseless on the touchline and haul them off down the tunnel. An Italian cameraman watches the scenes.

Meanwhile, back in England, an office television shows Sky Sports News airing footage of the incident. A large chair swivels around to reveal little Daniel Levy sitting in a grey suit, stroking a cat, with his little finger pressed to the corner of his mouth. He lets out an evil laugh.

Fredi Kanoute is writing his latest piece in his Icons diary

WHILE THE OTHERS are practising on the pitches of Spurs Lodge, Fredi is sitting on a bench tapping away on a laptop. He is thinking aloud to himself.

FK: Dear Diary, this will be the last time I speak to you. Mr Jol has told me to stop writing down my thoughts or he will break both my legs.

He thinks for a moment.

FK: I have been told to not be controversial any more

after announcing that the club wanted to get rid of me. So I will not be writing in detail this week about my plans to poison Mido, Andy Reid's big bones or the fact that Michael Carrick is in love with a Sky Sports News reporter. He's always giving him good 'quotes'.

He looks out at the players.

FK: Ah, screw it, they want me out anyway. What can I reveal to my loyal readers? Erm… Rodrigo Defendi's real name is Matt Spencer. He's from Peckham not Brazil. Frank Arnesen just thought it would impress everyone if one of his first signings was Brazilian. Come on people, he's a defender called Defendi, for goodness' sake. Have you ever heard him talk? Of course not, because he sounds like Rodney from *Only Fools and Horses*.

Also Noureddine Naybet is actually in his late forties but nobody seems to have cottoned on yet, despite the fact that he can't remember anyone's names and calls all the lads "son". Finally, Mr Jol has been signed up as the baddie in the new James Bond film…

He looks up and sees Martin staring at him from the training pitch. The big Dutchman starts to walk over.

FK: Oh crap.

He fumbles with the computer and manages to hit send. He throws the laptop at his manager and runs out of Spurs Lodge and is last seen running with his head down across the Essex countryside.

A day of interviews for the role of Spurs' new Sporting Director

DANIEL LEVY IS sitting in his office with Martin Jol alongside him as each applicant files in. First up is Sir Bobby Robson.

DL: Thank you for coming, Sir Bobby. So what can you do for Tottenham Hotspur?

Martin Jol introduces Teemu Tainio, Paul Stalteri, Tom Huddlestone, Aaron Lennon and Wayne Routledge at the start of the 2005-2006 season.

Ledley King holds the Peace Cup aloft after Spurs beat Lyon in the final.

The big man unveils The Pitbull

Portsmouth's Andy Griffin scores Spurs first goal of the season at Fratton Park.

Edgar David's shows Middlesbrough's Ray Parlour what he thinks of ex-Gooners.

Rob Styles leaves Spurs and Mido without a prayer against Chelsea.

Lee Young-Pyo makes his debut against Liverpool.

Robbie Keane can't be contained after coming to the rescue against Aston Villa.

BR: Well Sir Alan, I want a role in the new series of *The Apprentice*.

DL: Erm… I think you're a bit mixed up.

BR: I've still got it, lad. The faces, names and thoughts may be a little scrambled but I've still got it. Well, am I in the show or not?

DL. Erm… You're fired?

Sir Bobby walks out with a strangely satisfied smile on his face. David Pleat is next up but Martin Jol growls at him and he scurries back out the door. Sir Clive Woodward opens the door next but both men laugh and he turns around. Rodney Marsh, Arsène Wenger and Jeff Stelling all receive similar treatment.

It is late and Martin and Daniel are ready to pack it in for the day and begin to rise from their seats. Suddenly the door flies open and the room is bathed in white light. The two men shield their eyes. The voice of the late great Bill Nicholson booms around the four walls.

BN: It is better to fail aiming high than to succeed aiming low. And we of Spurs have set our sights very high, so high in fact that even failure will have in it an echo of glory.

The light is gone as soon as it came and the room returns to normal. Jol and Levy stare at each other. The buzz of the intercom on the chairman's desk makes them jump.

Intercom: Mr Levy, one more applicant has just turned up… a Mr Klinsmann. Shall I send him in?

DL: (Smiling) Yes please, Edna. We have a lot to talk about.

Chapter Two

August
And so it Begins

Saturday August 13th 2005

THE CROWDS ARE chanting, the new campaign's about to begin and the dressing room is full...

It's ten minutes until the whistle blows on the new Premiership season. The Spurs boys are sitting in the dressing room. Some have their heads down in deep concentration, others are talking among themselves. A few are watching Martin and Chris huddled in the corner in deep discussion.

The anticipation is dripping off the walls. The chants of the crowd are reverberating through the room. Andy Reid and Erik Edman nervously shuffle their feet and the sound of their studs raps on the floor. Then the pair in the corner turn. Everyone looks up and the room is silent.

Looming above them, Jol starts to talk. It's obvious he's been perfecting this speech for the last week. His words are steady, fluent and mesmerising. The message is clear. This is going to be our season. We've got the talent, we've got the energy, we've got the support, we've got the edge.

Jermain Defoe is watching his boss, letting the words flow through him. He already knows he's going to be a legend at Tottenham Hotspur and now he feels the supporters are going to witness something special from him today.

And so it Begins

The big Dutchman stops and the silence continues for a couple of seconds as each player digests their destiny. Wayne Routledge lets out a deep breath and looks at the ceiling. Selhurst Park was never like this. Teemu Tainio is smiling to himself; this is the club he was born to play for.

Suddenly Michael Dawson rises to his feet. He bangs his hands together and rallies the troops. The silence is broken and the time for action is nigh. They all stand. The nerves are gone, replaced by a passion. A passion for the cockerel, the club and the three points.

They all file out the door. The boss slaps them each on the back as they jog out. It's time for them to turn his tactics into domination. They are already lined up in the tunnel as the Portsmouth players stroll up alongside them. Sander Westerveld tries to wind up his opposing 'keeper, but it proves impossible. The England goalie is steely, determined and not in the mood for banter. He just stares at the Pompey player and looks back out towards the shining green pitch.

All the Spurs players are the same. Tainio and Routledge are peering ahead, trying to catch a glimpse of the thronging crowd. No false starts, they're both ready to fly out of the traps and never look back.

It's time. The lines begin to move and the players explode out into an eruption of noise. Names are booming around the stands. The syllables of Defoe, Mido and Carrick resound across the pitch. Even the Portsmouth players take a moment and stare at the enormous support roaring from the Lilywhite end of the stadium.

The twenty-two players take their places on the pitch. Jol and his right-hand Irishman take their seats in the dugout. Daniel Levy sits in the stand and looks down upon it all with expectation. Defoe and Mido stand over the ball in the centre circle, looking knowingly at each other. The referee checks his watch and puts the whistle to his lips.

The crowd goes silent and then the whistle sounds. A roar explodes from the terraces. Defoe grins at his strike partner before he touches the ball. It's time for the new era to begin…

Saturday August 13th 2005

FA Premiership
Portsmouth 0 Tottenham Hotspur 2
Attendance – 20,215
Spurs goalscorers: Griffin og, Defoe

Thursday August 18th 2005

THE PREMIERSHIP IS not even a week old and there's been enough activity at Tottenham Hotspur to power a small Vietnamese town for a year. A victory, familiar faces leaving with new names emerging on the horizon and an embarrassing international, featuring a couple of Lilywhites, thrown in for good measure – it's never quiet at White Hart Lane.

Let's start from the beginning. We went to Fratton Park on Saturday shorn of our star signing and our captain and our wee Irishman and we came away laughing at three points grabbed without much effort at all. Portsmouth showed all the class of a Jodie Marsh evening gown.

The sight of a suited Frenchman staring goggle-eyed at his team's lack of cutting edge must have sent a familiar shiver down the spines of the travelling Spurs fans. Thank Jacques he was in the opposition dugout this time for, Laurent Robert apart, the south coast team looked about as dangerous as a dead badger wearing comfortable slippers.

On the plus side for Spurs, Teemu Tainio had another

busy game and scared the pants off Viafara and Hughes. Never have heels and ankles been in so much danger of being bitten off during a football match. Paul Stalteri also looked solid on his debut, offering the bulk and tree trunk-legged tackle of Noe Pamarot with a touch more skill and attacking ability.

The legend that will be Wayne Routledge, however, looked a bit disappointing on a wet and windy day and he was often muscled off the ball. Had he finished an early Spurs move then perhaps things could have been different for him. There's not a lot more you can say about Jermain Defoe's finish that hasn't already been said. It was a typical poacher's goal and was enjoyed by Sven's henchman, Tord.

We had a few days' lull then yesterday what many suspected finally happened. Fredi Kanoute waved farewell to North London and packed his bags for sunny Seville. I freely admit to being extremely disappointed when Spurs were linked with the Malian two summers ago and enraged with him when he left for the African Nations Cup and once more when he played basketball for Liverpool in the Carling Cup quarter-final.

However, I wish him well on his travels and I'm sure he'll sleep easy knowing that I bear no grudge against him. The reason for that is not because he was essentially the hub of our creative play for much of last season or the fact that he slaps dollops of Pritt Stick on his ball-hugging chest when others dab on Vics vapour rub.

It's because he left Tottenham in a gracious and grateful manner. There were no Carrisms like "I'm leaving to win trophies" (always makes me laugh that one) or Simon Davies crowing about giving the best years of his career to Everton.

Fredi to his credit came out and said immediately: "I'm sad to be leaving Spurs but after I found out directly from the board they wanted to sell me I felt it was only right for me to leave.

"They have some very good players, but it's how they manage those players that I think will determine what they can achieve. Knowing how to deal with such a big squad is going to be their main issue this season – but if they can do that then I think they will have a great season."

While his displays may have split Spurs fandom, there's no doubt that the towering forward should receive an ovation if he ever returns to the Lane for a European match, even more so if he decides to handball in his own area.

As for incoming players, the usual suspects being touted are Dirk Kuyt or Kuijt depending on your side of the Channel, and Jermaine "I'm not a goldfish" Jenas. With the young Englishman you get the feeling that the goldfish bowl comments really mean: "I shudder every time I see Graeme Souness asking Alan Shearer for advice and then steaming in and injuring a player he doesn't like during a practice match."

As Spurs are obviously so set on securing the youngster this could mean one of four things. Firstly, does Daniel Levy want him at all costs because Arsenal were interested once, à la Carrick? Secondly, does Jol plan on playing a midfield with Routledge wide right and Carrick behind Jenas and Davids, with the left-footed Dutchman covering that side?

Perhaps it means that those three will play behind a front three of Routledge/Keane, Defoe and Mido? Or does it merely mean that we want to create our own version of Big Brother with Spurs Lodge becoming the home for our ten midfielders who have to live together and complete tasks to see who will play in each upcoming match.

Dirk Diggler is a different proposition entirely. The love child of Ian and Bob Dowie looks to be a battering ram of skilful proportions. Think Arnold Schwarzenegger with pace and ability. The 25-year-old scores goals from everywhere and unlike the much-heralded Kezman, has the physique to suit the English game. Once again his addition would be another step up for the squad level.

The final thought of the week has to take in the abomination that was last night's England game. There was a certain poetry about Sven taking off the two Spurs players and seeing the team fall apart before his eyes. Only in England could a fool like Calamity James continue to be picked for his national squad.

I don't know what irritates me more. The fact that he keeps making mistakes, that his Swedish lover keeps picking him or that without fail he will grin like an idiot after a footballing nightmare. Against Austria, he gurned like a clown after dropping one ball and last night he shook hands with a Danish player after the game while giggling like a cross-eyed schoolgirl.

How kind of him to announce later that he had not been prepared to come on as a sub. So how does that explain the other 3,240 errors in your career then, Davey boy? Only weeks after proclaiming he was ready to reclaim the role as England 'keeper, he showed that it would have been safer and less comical to stick Les Dennis between the sticks. Robbo must have been sitting on that bench crying with laughter. You can't pay for that sort of PR.

It was also nice to see that Jermain Defoe got the chance to build that relationship with Wayne Rooney that Sven said he was hoping to see. You can just imagine the egg-headed Swede in the dressing room at half-time taking Michael Owen aside and saying: "I can't bear it anymore. You complete me," then sending his child on.

Fair enough, Jermain looked nervous and too keen to come deep out of decent positions to collect the ball, the very thing Sven had wanted more of. However, to take him off at half-time in a friendly can only have confirmed to the young poacher that while the bespectacled one is the manager, he will never break into the first eleven on merit.

As for that second-half England side, I hope I'm not alone in finding it unbelievable that someone could pull on one of those white shirts and not want to die for the cause. Friendly or otherwise, those players are living the dream of millions of children and football-crazy men and at the very least they should seem grateful.

Saturday August 20th 2005

FA Premiership
Tottenham Hotspur 2 Middlesbrough 0
Attendance – 35,844
Spurs goalscorers: Defoe, Mido

Monday August 22nd 2005

THE TIME IS right to put the two brightest lights of the English game together on the national stage to form a mouth-watering partnership.

With Michael Owen sitting out through suspension, the time has come for Jermain Defoe to join Wayne Rooney up front against Wales next month and make it impossible for Sven to ditch him again.

First of all it has to be said that Michael Owen is a great player. Since his astonishing introduction to the world at the tender age of 18, he has gone on to become one of the most feared strikers in the world. However, there are now two younger strikers who are, to put it bluntly, even more terrifying for defenders.

While Owen sits on the Real Madrid bench watching his fellow Galacticos strut their stuttering stuff, Tottenham

Hotspur's Jermain Defoe has been straining at his England leash to attack international defences everywhere. His form for Spurs has been a cut above. While his club have started to look like going somewhere, he has been the driving force up front, creating goals often out of nothing. While Owen may be a slightly more tactically aware player than the young crowing cockerel, his pace has taken a knock or two with the recurring hamstring injuries.

At one point, he was forced to completely alter the way he ran to stop aggravating the injury. Not the best change to have to make when the previous style had brought with it lightning pace.

Defoe has that pace and with it comes a swaggering technical style which leaves defenders a step behind. He is as strong with his back to a defender as he is when running full-pelt towards him. Quick feet, lightning turns and shots taken early often mean that a half-chance is nestling in the goal before the 'keeper has a sniff of it.

The 22-year-old was finally given his first England start against Poland on September 8th, alongside team-mates Ledley King and Paul Robinson, and took his chance and then some. His opening goal, showcasing his touch and turning ability, was the toast of Sven, the players and the national media, although he wasn't allowed to mention that with a player media boycott.

On his prospective partner, you can't really add any more to the Wayne Rooney phenomenon. Like a juggernaut, the Manchester United striker has been smashing through records and newspaper headlines without any signs of slowing. Anyone that thought his injury in Euro 2004 may have knocked him back a bit would have been left slack-jawed at the sight of the best debut Old Trafford and probably the Premiership has ever seen.

While Owen loses his sharpness cosying up in those snug Bernabeu seats, the two youngsters are smashing in goals left, right and centre. If Defoe doesn't get his chance against Wales, it makes a mockery of everything the national side is meant to stand for. The team should be chosen on the current quality and form of the players. Picking Defoe and Rooney is no risk because they both now have that international experience and will have played against most of the Welsh defenders for their club sides.

If I were Danny Gabbidon or Robert Page on that Saturday afternoon in the Millennium Stadium, I'd be quaking in my boots if Sven decided on implementing one of his rare media-friendly decisions and played those two terrifyingly in-form strikers.

Wednesday August 24th 2005

FA Premiership
Blackburn Rovers 0 Tottenham Hotspur 0
Attendance – 22,375

Friday August 26th 2005

HI THERE, MY name's Alasdair and yes I'm a footyholic. The realisation finally hit me at 1.45am this morning when I caught my reflection in a window, standing shivering in front of a tiny kitchen television watching Channel 5's Dutch football just to scout a potential Spurs signing.

I had woken up at about 1.20am with a well-read copy of *The Miracle of Castel Di Sangro* congealed to my face. Wearing only a faded pair of Klinsmann-era Spurs shorts, I braved the draughts sweeping through my parents' old house to grab a glass of water from downstairs.

And so it Begins

In a dopey daze, I flicked on the tiny kitchen television while glugging down the drink. Without my contact lenses I could just make out the forms of footballers on the screen. Leaning with my nose practically touching the screen, I discovered it was a re-run of the Sparta–Feyenoord derby game from Sunday featuring a certain Dirk Kuyt.

The home side were a goal up. I'd only planned to scan the channels briefly but I ended up staying in that awkward frozen pose for the next hour watching the power and pace of the blonde-haired monster battling away up front. Defenders bounced off him this way and that. He won every header to be won and then came his moment just before half-time.

The muscular target man found himself in space in the box with almost the last kick of the half and lashed the ball past the gloriously named Rene Ponk in the Sparta goal. The equaliser broke the home side's morale and they returned from the break a shell of their first-half selves. Surrounded by darkness, I eventually turned off the small screen, having watched the match end 3-1 to Feyenoord. I was frozen, aching but happy. Kuyt was impressive and his power, matched with close control, will suit the Premiership.

So I went back to bed and lay there awake thinking about how much of my life is given over to football. How many hours are left in a week after you take out travelling to White Hart Lane, watching live English and Spanish games on Sky, Premiership Plus matches, Italian games on Eurosport, Football First, *Match of the Day, Soccer AM, Gillette Soccer Saturday*, flicking through Teletext and the greatest channel ever invented, Sky Sports News?

How many football fans can honestly say they've sat for an hour in front of satellite television without feeling the urge to flick over to Sky Sports News to check if something amazing is scrolling in the yellow bar across the bottom? Goodbye family, goodbye social life, hello lonely bliss.

It's not just a home vice either. I've no doubt that if my boss knew how much of my nine-hour working day I spend surfing the internet for Spurs rumours and spurious gossip, I'd either be sacked on the spot or ordered in at weekends to make up the years of overtime. Work is such an obtrusion.

This week has been a particularly difficult one. I've been whisked away by my family to spend seven days at my parents' home in Kilmarnock, just outside Glasgow, with orders to survive without my intravenous drip of the beautiful game.

Although my father shares my fascination with football, for some reason he's far happier watching a game unravel on the sensory explosion that is Teletext than splashing out on Sky. So I've had to sit up here with only Gary and his *Match of the Day* for company. Good behaviour has earned me a couple of five-minute internet peeks in the mornings and the time to write this piece. Guess who's wearing the trousers this week.

The fiercely patriotic Scottish newspapers up here revel in the 'thrills' of Rangers and Celtic clashes with perhaps a paragraph left over for news from south of the border, unless a side has a Scot in their ranks and then they might earn an extra few lines in gratitude.

I managed to win a few hours respite' to listen to the game via the internet on Wednesday night although there was little point. I'm sure I heard the "umms" and "errs" of Santini whispering in the wind as the mighty Spurs rained down one furious shot on goal. After last year's away form, though, it could still be seen as a point gained rather than two dropped and our unbeaten record is intact, as is the big fat zero in our goals conceded column.

In keeping with my week of abstinence, I'll be driving back home to England tomorrow while my beloved Lilywhites take on Chelski. I can only hope that Radio 5 is covering the game and I can spend the 90 minutes far past the coverage-killing hills and valleys of Lancashire.

Despite Wednesday's boredom and my distance from the match tomorrow, I'm actually quite confident about our chances. It's about time the wheels came off the Russian money train and there's no reason why it can't happen at White Hart Lane tomorrow. I think Martin Jol will have been disappointed at Wednesday's performance and will make sure in his own special way that the players are at a different level for Chelsea. Cue some headlocks and beatings at Spurs Lodge.

Michael Carrick will be fresh, as will Jermain Defoe. Davids shouldn't be tired after his brief stroll around Ewood Park. If anything, it was another half an hour or so to acclimatise to the English game. Was anyone else impressed by seeing him screaming at Mido, on *Match of the Day*, to get off the pitch quicker for his arrival? The man is desperate to win and I keep having this vision of him scaring the crap out of Lampard within the first minute at the Lane with a crunching challenge.

So I'm hopeful about tomorrow, about my team and the fact that I'll be returning soon to my bubble of football life. I suspect I'm not the only person with this addiction and I hope I'm not the last. As I said before, my name is Alasdair, I'm a footyholic and you know what? I just love it.

Saturday August 27th 2005

FA Premiership
Tottenham Hotspur 0 Chelsea 2
Attendance – 36,077

Sunday August 28th 2005

RATHER THAN THE easy task of checking me out of Princess Alexandra Hospital's cardiac ward, which is the case after most Spurs games, my family faced the indignity of bailing me out of Harlow Police Station last night after I went on a drunken rampage through the town starting at approximately 4.45pm.

Two officers arrested me in the park howling at the moon: "Just beat Chelski for once, you bastards!" After my £1.38 bail was paid, I returned home and slept it all off in the bath. I am still to have a wave of perspective wash over me; the closest I've come was when my wife turned the shower on my head to wash the beer out of my hair as I mumbled about Rob Styles.

As always, with an optimist like me, there is something to cling to. I was reading on Saturday morning about Sir Alex Ferguson's time at Manchester United. It struck me how passionate the grumpy Scot was about his team from the word go.

I hope it is no coincidence that our own Jol marched into that boardroom within minutes of his appointment to give a chest-thumping speech to board members detailing his quest to bring the glory glory days back to Tottenham.

He still seems to have the passion and on the bench always seems to be kicking every ball with the players. From what this season has already brought, he would seem to have the necessary motivational skills to kick the team up the backside. Think of him as Kevin Keegan with a grasp of tactics.

I know it's frustrating and I'm as impatient as the next man, but remember we've all signed on for the ride, however long it takes. We are all Tottenham Hotspur though and through. I know my blood is white and blue. We're not prawn sandwich-munching supporters picking a team across the country to support because they're playing well. This is something different in the history of our club, a seismic shift, and we have to give it a chance to evolve fully.

What would come of revolutions if they ended after a few months because the army withdrew its support? The players on that pitch are ultimately our pawns in battle. Slaughter them and they will wither and surrender; get behind them, give them your full supporting roar and although we may lose a few battles on the way, we will win this war. Phew, there was that perspective... just in time.

Chapter Three

September
Martin, Mariners and Moaning

Wednesday September 7th 2005

FOR THE FIRST time in my budding journalism career, I was shocked. The local paper I work for wanted me to cover something involving Tottenham Hotspur. After my editor dragged me back to consciousness by throwing pencils at my face for a couple of minutes, I was told I'd be covering the Spurs XI friendly against Bishop's Stortford.

Despite working up the road from Stortford's Woodside Park, it was the first time I had visited the Nationwide Conference South club's ground. It was the ideal way to put the first team's last match out of my mind and Mido's truly awful sending off by Tottenham's best friend Rob Styles. Oh, what could have been?

Anyway, I was swept up to the little stadium's press box with my son and a mate who were cunningly disguised as notepads. As I took my place next to the match reporter for Spurs' official website, I spied a Dowie out the corner of my eye.

It wasn't Iain but his brother Bob, Crystal Palace's director of football, who was sitting across the aisle. I frantically tried to work out who he was watching. Was it Mounir El-Hamdaoui who was playing up front, was it

Phillip Ifil or Tom Huddlestone in the back four or was he even lining up a shock move for Sean Davis who was starting in the middle?

As my son, Ryan, was straining at the leash to get his autograph, I let him go in the hope that the director might reveal some prize information. The suited Bob, however, did nothing of the sort and proceeded in a charming manner to try to convert the kid to the ways of the Eagles. In disgust I yelled for the boy to come back as the match was about to start and glared at Bob.

The line-up for Spurs saw Forecast in goal, with Ifil, Huddlestone, McKie and Daniels at the back. Davis lined up alongside McKenna in the centre with O'Hara and Maghoma cutting inside from the wings. Mounir started in attack alongside the blonde-quiffed Barnard.

So I guess you'd think that from the kick-off a Premiership player like Davis would boss the game. In fact he didn't at all, choosing to sit in front of the back four and let the energetic young McKenna do all the work in midfield. The 19-year-old didn't disappoint and it wouldn't be far off to compare his aggressive, pitch-covering style to that of first-teamer Teemu Tainio.

In fact, he opened the scoring on 16 minutes, having picked up the ball on the halfway line, driving forward before curling a delicious 25-yard shot into the top right-hand corner past the helpless Stortford 'keeper.

Although the Spurs youngsters dominated the possession, Stortford hit back against the run of play with a crisp passing move that put debutant Julian Edwards, a new signing from Chelmsford, through to fire past Forecast. Within eight minutes Spurs were ahead again, however, after Barnard headed home a delightful hanging Ifil cross.

The young right-back looked impressive going forward during the game although he was admittedly caught out a few times at the back by the Stortford front two. In fact, he often had a better end product in the final third than Jacques Maghoma on the right wing, who had a particular obsession with stepovers. Although his dribbling got him into the box occasionally, his crossing caused few problems for anyone but a group of rowdy youngsters behind the goal.

Huddlestone looked composed and strong at the back, frequently dribbling the ball effortlessly past onrushing attackers or smashing them aside with his frighteningly towering frame. I've never seen an 18-year-old of that stature in my life. The term man-mountain seems inadequate somehow.

As well as scaring away small children and animals, he also delivered some fine cross-field passes to set up waves of attacks from the right and left. On the downside, attackers with a turn of pace were able to get by him on occasions, although I'm hoping that could be attributed to his recovering knee injury.

The North London side took the 2-1 lead into half-time and El-Hamdaoui did not appear for the second half. It was also interesting to note that Bob Dowie left shortly into the second half having failed to convert my family to the ways of the Palace. Take from that what you will. I certainly speculated wildly with my friend and those around me about the object of his affection among the Spurs contingent.

After the break Lee Barnard put away a penalty when Jamie O'Hara was bundled over just inside the area. However, a disastrous three-minute spell for the Spurs back four soon evened the scores with a header from Richard Howell, as he was challenged by two flailing defenders, and a Rob Gillman shot on the turn.

Normal service was resumed with McKenna, substitute Radwan Hamed and Jamie O'Hara all scoring, stamping

Spurs' authority back on the game before Stortford sub Sam Adejokun delivered a final reply with a smart finish.

As the game ended, I headed down the tunnel after the players and stood in the entrance of the Spurs dressing room alongside the club's journalist. We stood awkwardly as Clive Allen ripped into his young side for what he rightly saw as a poor defensive display from a team containing three top players and an array of young talent. I decided against grabbing the legendary goalscorer as he led the team from the dressing room for their post-match warm-down. This was probably due to the fact that his face showed about as much joy as those few souls at the Frank Arnesen fan club's annual dinner on Sunday.

The players completed their routine and signed autographs for the throng of waiting kids, with Sean Davis kindly giving his training top to one widow and daughter of a Spurs and Stortford fan who died recently. After that touching moment, I took the opportunity to join the Spurs press man as he pinned Clive Allen against a wall with his Dictaphone.

I introduced myself and shook the hand of the now smiling man I'd watched lash in goal after goal as a youngster. To say my heart was smashing into my ribcage was an understatement as I put my questions to Clive and tried to keep up with the answers with my shorthand. Mental note for next time: notepads are for dummies, Dictaphones are for champions.

He wasn't happy with the performance, saying: "It was like a cup tie. We gave Bishop's Stortford the chances to get back into the game. It was an interesting one and I'm sure we'll get many like this. It's all part of the learning curve for the players.

"They need to look at the game and learn a lot from it. There were negatives to take. It was an important match for a lot of them and it is all part of their learning."

On the withdrawal of Mounir at half-time he would only say: "It was planned that he would come off and he showed no ill effects from his injury. Obviously it was good for Sean and Tom to come through 90 minutes." He didn't comment on whether the striker had come off to save him for the bench on Saturday but that didn't stop me thinking that as I scribbled.

On his lower league opponents he said: "I was impressed with the tempo and the quality of their finishing was to their credit. There were certain times when we may have helped them out when we've given the ball away.

"I was speaking to Martin Hayes before the game and I know the home results haven't been what he wanted. However, if they play in that way in the future I certainly think they'll get into gear."

Then it was done. Clive had to go. Yes, he's Clive now. We may never share a pint in friendship but I've met him and we'll always be on first-name terms in my slightly-warped mind. He came across as a friendly guy who is very passionate about ensuring the youngsters at the club have the best possible chance of making it in the professional game.

So I left the small ground with a smile on my face, a son with a pad full of autographs and a satisfied mate and we drove off into the night. The car screeched to a halt just past the car park gates with the words "Dad, can I like Crystal Palace too?" Damn you Bob Dowie, damn you.

Saturday September 10th 2005

FA Premiership
Tottenham Hotspur 0 Liverpool 0
Attendance – 36,148

Monday September 12th 2005

WHEN THE CURTAIN fell on Spurs' season in May, I would have gladly taken a five-place improvement on the previous campaign as well as another seven points. In fact, I'd probably have bitten the hand, arm and shoulder off whoever offered that prospect, but you know what? I'd unwittingly become a player in Bill Nicholson and the Shawshank Redemption.

Let me introduce myself: most folks call me Never Red. I spent most of my days in Shawshank sitting in my cell, dreaming of Europe and the success which lay outside these dreary walls. It had been a warm and stormy summer, but at least I was safe in the knowledge that my parole was coming up in a year or two and my life would soon change for the better.

I was almost happy to wait out the remainder of my time alongside all my fellow inmates, packed inside the looming stadium watching busloads of new souls coming in every window, betting between ourselves which one would crack first.

I think it was sometime in mid-November last year when the new guy was brought in. Little did I know then that this giant of a man had come to turn my world upside down. Most folks didn't think the tall newcomer in a suit would make it through that first match. Anyone who's ever been in Shawshank will tell you that that first one is always the hardest. But he made it through and earned a lot of people's respect that day.

As the days drew on, we soon realised that Martin Jol wasn't like the others. He wasn't content with sitting around waiting for things to happen. Everyone liked him; even some of the less aggressive stewards took to his charming manner.

Then one day he came to me and said that he'd heard

I was the guy who could get anything for a price. The big man wanted me to get him Bill Nicholson. It was the strangest request I'd ever had but I managed to pull a few strings and within a month, a large poster of the managerial legend was adorning his wall.

Martin and I became good friends over the following months. I could tell he wasn't content with the mediocrity of the place and his enthusiasm rubbed off on all of us. Then two weeks ago I found out what he'd been up to the whole time.

Behind his revered image of Bill Nicholson, he'd been digging a way out – an escape route away from the tedium and the predictability. I was torn. I'd been expecting to get out anyway in a year or so but now this new guy was offering me a way out immediately. Half of me patiently whispered that I'd been waiting for decades to be released, so what difference would another season or two make?

But I was seduced by Martin's plans and his quick way out. I was tired of years of nothing but boredom, lifted only by observing the newcomers being brought in every summer. So that night, we hatched plans to escape the following Saturday.

At about 3pm on that hot afternoon, we carefully crawled under the poster and began our daring journey. Only two hours in, disaster struck. A pile of red bricks had caved in halfway along the tunnel and blocked our path. There was, however, a chink of light at the top of the blockage but we knew the adventure would have to be postponed at least for today. After we had crawled back to his cell, feeling none too happy, Martin and I decided to meet up again the next Sunday to give it one last go.

A week passed and we met up to give it one last shot. I could see that some of the hope had drained from my partner's face but there was always that slim chance. Once down the tunnel, we struggled to lift the heavy blocks. Each seemed to weigh more than the last. Just when it looked as if we were finally getting somewhere we heard the barking of dogs. My bald partner-in-crime stopped dead, as did I.

Through the cracks in the pile we saw him. It was the skinny, squinting warden flanked by his Gallic captain with his lips curled into a smirk. The prison dogs were going crazy and for a moment I turned and came eye to eye with my towering friend. We knew that this daring escape was over before we'd even made it out of Shawshank.

As I sit here in my cell this evening contemplating the future, I couldn't be much more depressed. Hopefully in time my thoughts will clear and I'll realise that it won't be long until I reach the success that lies outside. I feel it's my and my friend's destiny. I saw him today in the canteen. He was hunched over his food, not talking to anyone. Just as I was about to pass him, though, he caught my eye and from beneath that dour exterior, he smiled mischievously.

I get the feeling it won't be long before our paths cross again, outside the confines of these walls. It's been a long wait but as the days count down I find I'm growing more and more excited. I think it's the excitement that only a hopeful man can feel, turning a corner towards the end of a long journey in which the conclusion is looking brighter.

I hope Martin is there at the end.

I hope to see my friend and shake his hand.

I hope the Premiership trophy is as gleaming as it has been in my dreams.

I hope.

Saturday September 17th 2005

FA Premiership
Aston Villa 1 Tottenham Hotspur 1
Attendance – 33,686
Spurs goalscorer: Keane

Monday September 19th 2005

DEAR MARTIN

I am writing this brief letter to you because I am a very sad man. We are six games into the season now and for some reason Spurs are not top of the league. Could you please explain why?

I expect an answer to this note as I have supported the side for 26 years now and everyone from Keith Burkinshaw to Glenn Hoddle has replied. The only one that didn't was a certain Frenchman and he resigned a couple of days after I sent my second letter. Don't make me send a second one. Nobody likes the second one.

So as I was saying, I was allowed into the computer room today and I noticed that there are seven teams above my beloved Tottenham Hotspur in the Premiership. You have had a whole ten months to shape the team and I am distinctly unhappy with the progress made.

Someone told me today that we have only lost one game so far and conceded three goals with the third best defence in the league. After nutting the bringer of bad news, I shouted: "Third best! We are not a team that settles for third best." I don't care if we let in five goals a game as long as we score six with some sexy football.

I am similarly unimpressed with your new signings. Who is this Grzegorz Rasiak bloke? My father told me never to trust anyone with the letter Z in their name.

That was just before he was arrested for trying to strangle Zsa Zsa Gabor. You can maybe understand why I am slightly perturbed by this Polish giant.

He is taller than the butler from the Addams Family and he's hardly the kind of pin-up we need at the Lane. In my letter to Daniel Levy in June, I expressly requested a poster-boy Beckhamesque marketable commodity. Even more irritatingly he is neither Dutch nor Brazilian nor a wonderkid. Do you not play Football Manager or the computer management games? If you wish I could send you a list of potential stars.

I have been distinctly unimpressed with the Pole's efforts in his two games thus far. His disallowed 'goal', hitting the post and the flick in the build-up to the equaliser on Saturday aside, what has he done? I very much doubt I'm alone in thinking that aerial ability and link-up play is not enough for a modern-day striker. We need goals. Get that Kanoute bloke back. Now he was a poacher.

I have similar concerns over Wayne Routledge and Aaron Lennon who are too injured and too small respectively. Lennon looks like a tiny child and I have been afraid of children ever since I saw *The Omen*. At one point during the Chelsea match he stopped and stared at me through my television screen and next thing I knew all these birds were attacking me. He's an evil Oompa Loompa, that Aaron. His name starts with the same letter twice for goodness sake.

As for Jenas, he's 22 already, he's passed his peak. What more can he learn? It's hardly like he's got some world-class superstar alongside him to soak up knowledge from, is it? Not to mention it's a little greedy to have another England international in the ranks. I think you've wasted your money, Martin.

That Lee's all right though. He does pretty tricks that

make me smile. I can't tell from looking at him if he's 38, 28 or 18, but I wouldn't care if he was the inventor kid from the Goonies, he's all right by me.

I have also decided that although I slated Robbie Keane over the summer for not signing a new contract and his inability to score simple tap-ins, he scored a goal at the weekend, whereas Jermain did not. Therefore he should start every game from now on. I trust you will agree with me.

So what happens next, Martin? I understand we are two points better off than we would have been from the same six fixtures last season, but that doesn't cut any ice with me. I lived through the glory of Ossie Ardiles' famous five; did you think I'd be delighted with two measly points?

I expect us to beat Grimsby by at least six goals tomorrow night and Fulham by three on Monday. If we do that then maybe, just maybe, I will praise every player on that pitch, you will be my god once again and I'll believe we can finally win that elusive league title. If not then I'm afraid your job may be on the line.

Oh and I almost forgot, can you send your reply in an envelope with rounded edges as the staff here often do not pass on mail with sharp corners as they think I will harm myself. I think they're being overprotective but them's the rules.

I look forward to hearing from you soon,

Fred Fickle
(Come on you Spurs)

Tuesday September 20th 2005

Carling Cup
Grimsby 1 Tottenham Hotspur 0
Attendance – 8,206

Wednesday September 21st 2005

THE PAIN OF last night is still so fresh, I'm not sure I should even try and put anything down on a page. I fear that whatever emerges from my fingertips will cause small children to cry and grown men to run screaming from the room.

Sorry kids, avert your eyes, I can't stop myself! Grimsby! Bloody Grimsby! Aargh! Must stop writing. Pain too much. Eyes blurring over in utter frustration and disgust. Must fight the urges of Fred Fickle to send a 75-page letter to the big man.

What pains me even more than the loss and the crappy last-minute goal was the fact that we were made to look like a bunch of complete plonkers with one of our strongest elevens on the pitch. The accompanying irony is that a younger, hungrier fringe team would probably have comfortably disposed of the Mariners by half-time.

Despite the fact that we have a squad of 74 players, we prodded most of our finest onto that pitch of humiliation. Teams below us in the Premiership with smaller squads sent out reserve and youth sides and got through, yet we strode out there with our pants down just asking to be spanked.

We sent out a team of 11 highly paid stars onto a bumpy pitch on a cold and windy evening, each wide-eyed player looking as if they had got off at the wrong stop and missed their mummy. The Grimsby players must have seen the glittering array of Premiership names, including five England players and ten internationals among their ranks, and thought, "Bloody hell, it's just like watching *Match of the Day*! Let's prove we can mix it with this bunch."

They probably looked at Michael Carrick shivering in

the centre circle in his long sleeves and knew all they had to do was give us a battle. Their towering centre backs must have laughed at the vertically challenged front pairing of Robbie Keane and Jermain Defoe as they held them back with a mere hand to the forehead.

It wasn't just our lack of fight on the night, it was our lack of creativity. If we can't create enough decent chances against a League Two side, what chance do we have against Fulham in our next game? It was Paul Robinson who had the busier night out of the two 'keepers, having to pull off a number of saves. He's the only man I will give any credit to in a Lilywhite shirt.

It was one of those horrible/magical nights that cup upsets are drawn to like moths to a flame as some pop star with a conical bra once said. Rubbish conditions, overconfident, overpaid footballers and a lower league team flying high with the confidence and chemistry of being top of their division.

I disappeared for hours after the game and was apparently spotted later last night by a dog-walking pensioner, who told the police of a strange man on Hackney Marshes howling obscenities at the moon. I awoke naked in my garden this morning with a ripped Spurs shirt between my teeth.

Fearing a reoccurrence, I'm going to finish it there today and keep it short, sharp and not particularly sweet. Anything else I could possibly say on the matter would require the use of ridiculous amounts of swearwords, the like of which would make even Bernard Manning blush. Time to consign this defeat to the drawer marked 'Cock-ups of the Rich and Famous'. Goodnight cruel world, I'm off to resume my crying.

Sunday September 25th 2005

AS I'M SEEING out the tail end of last week's tantrum, I'm going to take a look at the Premiership itself rather than that team I still admittedly love.

A scandal has rocked the division this season and for once it has nothing to do with overpaid players battering each other or inviting young women into hotel rooms.

The Greatest League in the World™ has been slapped well and truly in the face by the allegation that it has in fact become rather boring. The nation's newspapers have been flooded with different facts and figures declaring that this campaign has been the worst in recent memory.

Liverpool's early season bore draw against Manchester United, two of the supposedly best teams in the land, sent masses of armchair fans to sleep as journalists pounded on their laptops in frustration.

A certain tabloid newspaper even gave £10,000 to young Aston Villa striker Luke Moore when he ended their campaign this weekend to get someone to score the first goal against Chelsea. It took 641 minutes of football for the ball to find its way into the champions' net and they still ended up winning the match.

Is it just about the marauding leaders though? After only six games of the campaign, suicidal statisticians have been keen to point out that, compared with 163 goals at the same stage in 2003/04 and 144 last term, the ball has crossed the line a mere 112 times this season.

Why the drop? Is the soccer being played less creative? Has Chelsea's contagious and stifling 4-5-1 formation increased the number of goalless draws or 1-0 wins and decreased the excitement? Are the promoted teams better equipped this year to take on the rigours of the league and less likely to receive a 4-0 spanking? Have the players lost touch with the supporters? Are 11am kick-offs to suit television killing crowds?

There's a lot of opinion, but two of the most prevalent suggestions offered by the fans and the experts are that the steep rise in ticket prices is keeping supporters away and the torrent of televised games is keeping them at home. The view from the nation's streets, or my Spurs-supporting mates, says it all.

"With plasma screen TVs, surround sound and instant replays from angles you never thought existed, is it a surprise that people don't want to spend £50 to sit in a cold corner of a stadium with a restricted view, when they could be at home in a chair shouting abuse and demented joy in almost equal measure?" said David Craggs (28), of St Albans.

Rob Parker (45), of Leicester, added: "Teams have realised they can't play big teams with flowing, fast paced football and expect to come away with anything so they have adapted their tactics to counter. This may ensure the likes of Bolton, Charlton and Wigan do better over the season, but over 90 minutes it isn't the most thrilling spectacle to watch."

"There was a time when football was for the fans. Now we're just part of the spectacle. We're taken for granted. They think we'll just show up and watch any old game. The football clubs need to start thinking about us again," said 23-year-old Michael Russell.

Another mate, 39-year-old Mark from California, drew comparisons with MLS, saying: "Are the same reasons for the decline in attendances in English soccer the same that explain why a true strong home soccer league can't make it big in the US? Television ultimately has the greater economic control not the clubs.

"The supporters have become consumers of the all branded sporting experience product – and are less and less true fans. Slowly and surely the greater disillusionment of the overpaid superstars keeps us at home, talking about them in virtual contexts."

Ticket prices vary wildly in the Premiership from club to club, with costs generally higher at the London clubs. Tottenham offer the top seat price at £70 while their cheapest ticket is among the league's lowest at £26. Newcomers Wigan's prices range from £25 to a mere £17.

After almost a quarter of this season, nine sides have seen a decline in their average attendance from the same point last year, while the number of live matches to be televised on Sky this term has increased from 106 to 138.

However, the chief executive of the Premier League, Richard Scudamore, has rejected claims that the league is in trouble and said that TV coverage should not be criticised, calling it "the rocket fuel that sent the Premier League into the stratosphere".

While he revealed that the Premiership's average attendance was up on last season, he was worried enough to set up a working group to investigate the issue for the remainder of the season.

Rooney, Gerrard, Lampard, Henry, Davids et al would certainly disagree that the English game has become boring. Many within the footballing world resent this year's fad to knock the beautiful game.

By seizing on a few clubs' slightly lower figures and a few dull matches, have the media missed out on something? As Jimmy Greaves said, football truly is "a funny old game". It only takes a moment of magic to reignite a match, a crowd of thousands or even a season. Perhaps it's better to wait until the campaign's final whistle before hammering that final nail into the English Premiership.

Monday September 26th 2005

FA Premiership
Tottenham Hotspur 1 Fulham 0
Attendance – 35,427
Spurs goalscorer: Defoe

Thursday September 29th 2005

AFTER GETTING BACK to winning ways following a torrid couple of weeks, I was wondering whether anyone else had taken a moment to consider what it must be like to support another club?

No serious change of loyalty, of course, rather just wonder what it would have been like had there been no Tottenham Hotspur. Would there be more or fewer thrills and spills?

The fact that I was immediately wrapped in a white blanket, bearing the cockerel and ball, as soon as I was born meant that a hefty portion of my life was destined to be handed over to the White Hart Lane outfit. I never had a choice although I hope I would have chosen the same path had fate asked the question.

I never wondered whether the pitch was greener on the other side, even with the realisation as successive campaigns ended that all that pre-season euphoria had been rather misplaced. No questions even as I sat during the angriest hours of a week-long sulk, stabbing the oversized ears of a David Pleat voodoo doll, after ten-men Manchester City made that FA Cup comeback.

Would anyone swap the highs and lows of a side always seemingly on the cusp of something for one that was regularly at the top or another struggling to survive each season? I personally have a lot of respect for people who have stuck with their local side through hell and

Grimsby's Jean-Paul Kamudimba Kalala scores the most embarrassing goal of the season.

Robbie Keane performs his trademark cartwheel after completing a sensational comeback against Charlton at The Valley.

Jermaine Jenas celebrates after sending a stunning free-kick past Manchester United's Edwin Van der Sar.

Teemu Tainio leaves the North London derby after getting the elbow from Sol Campbell.

Ledley King leaves 'you know who' floudering while heading past Jens Lehmann at the Lane.

Spurs past and present clash as Teddy Sheringham and Edgar Davids discuss matters.

Michael Brown tells Jermain Defoe he needs to get off the bench against Middlesbrough to impress Sven.

West Brom's Kanu steals a small child after scoring two goals against Spurs at The Hawthorns.

high water, foregoing the glory of the Premiership.

There's a lot to be said for a supporter who regularly travels to watch Oxford United getting beaten most weeks in League Two because that's the side he was meant to follow. The same goes for those turning out to watch Wigan, Norwich or Crystal Palace.

It must be wonderful to see your side rise through the divisions and surface in the top league. However, there must be a certain depressing air of inevitability about falling back down a rung on the money-clad ladder and always losing your top stars, although to be fair Wigan have started well enough.

On the other end of the scale, what must it be like to support a team which will always be at the top or thereabouts each year? I count a Manchester United fan among my friends and he admitted a little while ago that during his side's golden years last decade, despite the trophies, it did get slightly less exciting with each successive year. As with players who have won most things, he said the fans found themselves targeting a certain trophy, i.e. The Champions League, over the league title coming home again.

For Spurs fans, that's a bizarre concept as many would be happier than Jose in a room full of roubles if we had lifted the League Cup this season. In a recent interview, Fabio Cappello, the Juventus manager, said: "I once said 'I'll never coach Juventus', because they are one of those teams who often win and I was worried that it is normal for them to win." The fact that vast amounts of money thrown at his face changed his mind doesn't mean the statement stops working for the ordinary fan on the street.

I guess it depends on the type of person you are. How many people start a football management or Pro-Evolution style computer game as a top club or one they can build upon? I'm definitely in the latter camp as I love the challenge. However, I have known people to start as Chelsea, not change the team, and win everything easily. Where's the fun in that?

The same applies to fandom. As much pain as supporting Spurs brings me on occasions, the eternal hope that we will eventually return to former glories gives me far greater enjoyment. The media seize on these expectations and I very much doubt any other club enjoys as frenzied and exciting summers and transfer windows as this particular North London club. What other supporters would keep refreshing their official club website's homepage up to and past midnight on September and February 1st? We expect deadline deals and the Tottenham officials invariably deliver.

As much as it pains some Spurs fans, we are firmly in that 'sexy' group of teams aiming for that next level including 'luminaries' such as Middlesbrough, Aston Villa and Bolton. At least, if you stopped a small child playing football in a street in Brazil or Argentina and asked him which of the four clubs he had heard of, the answer would always be: "Tottingham Hotspur."

What happens when Spurs eventually break into that top three/four, I hear you ask? Will supporting the Lilywhites become a lesser experience? My only answer to that is that I think our adventure is only just beginning. We still have to taste Europe again and consistent success and trophy-lifting in the style of Manchester United certainly won't be achieved in the next five years, whatever our aspirations or expectations.

Who knows what this season holds? It could be one of glory, building or disaster. We have the ability to breach the top four for the first time but we could quite rightly be happy with a place in the Uefa Cup, which would be another step on the journey. There's always the chance that something could go wrong along the way. Who would have thought that Jacques 'Stay back Erik' Santini or Frank 'Show me the money' Arnesen would have left so quickly?

Very rarely does a pundit's preview of an upcoming Spurs match omit the term 'false dawn'. As glorious as our past has been, it has always loomed ominously behind the shuffling line of subsequent nervous managers who have each failed to escape being swallowed up.

Like Indiana Jones running from the rolling boulder at the beginning of *Raiders of the Lost Ark*, the enormous aura of 'Sir' Bill Nicholson has crushed successors standing terrified in its wake. Here's hoping that a giant called Martin is the man to catch the boulder, hoist it onto his shoulders and carry the ball of hopes and dreams onwards.

Chapter Four

October
The Comeback Kings

Saturday October 1st 2005

FA Premiership
Charlton Athletic 2 Tottenham Hotspur 3
Attendance – 27,111
Spurs goalscorers: King, Mido, Keane

Tuesday October 4th 2005

AS I LIE here on my sickbed with family members popping their heads around the door only to gasp at my state, throw in some paracetamol and run towards a group of men in white overalls and masks who hose them down, I have been thinking about those over the years who have lost the love of the Spurs faithful.

Football is a sprawling global pantomime and each player must play their part on the enormous stage. There are the heroes who dive in at the far post to save the day and the villains who come out of nowhere with a sly handball, foul or just a distinct lack of ability.

There's not just the media-hyped Robbie Savages of the show. Within each club is a supporting cast member who never fails to make an audience member roll their eyes when his name appears on the teamsheet.

I'm not talking about the Campbells and Carrs who left the team by choice and incurred our wrath but those players who dare not live up to our expectations. Like all fans, there have been a band of men who arrived at White Hart Lane with everything going for them and then lost it before our very eyes.

The corridors of the stadium are littered with the carcasses of those who didn't make it. The other day, I watched a cleaner sweep Jose Dominguez, Moussa Saib and Kazuyuki Toda into a dustpan. Ah little Jose; he arrived in 1997 as a mini-me version of Ricky Villa and David Ginola. How I cheered and whooped as he ran headlong towards the opposition in his first few games.

Unfortunately it didn't take long to realise that that was all the little guy did. He ran as fast as he could into defenders' legs. The boy had skills but whenever he saw an opposing player it was like a red rag to a bull and the head went down and he just charged. There was nothing quite as bizarre as Jose bouncing into the crowd off the thigh of another meaty full-back.

Soon his inclusion would send a shudder down my · spine, as would the names of Saib and Toda on the back of a matchday programme.

In their own countries they were heroes; in the Premiership they looked as scared as the soon-to-be Colleen Rooney does when Wayne flashes a flirtatious smile at another passing pensioner. Between them, Saib and Toda amassed a staggering five starts and 12 substitute appearances for Spurs. Strange, as the newspaper reports assured me when they signed that they were both "highly rated".

There are scores of others: my personal list of blasts from the past includes Justin 'A lack of skill won't stop me' Edinburgh and his adopted sons, Mauricio Tarrico and Paulo Tramezzani. Everyone has their own pet hates and those that really wind them up no matter what good they do.

Ode to Jol

It's quite disturbing what lengths football fans can go to in their hatred of certain players. I have certainly been known to build massive bonfires in my garden and out of the five players I have disposed of, only Ramon Vega's family have so far filed a missing persons report.

The outpouring of hatred can be massive but deep down most fans know that it is all part of the pantomime. Although I hate jeering of players during matches, I guess it comes as part of the required booing and hissing of the villains of the piece. That doesn't mean it does any good though.

However, once in a while, one of those no-hopers turns it around and becomes an unlikely cult hero. One that springs instantly to mind is the sainthood given to Ronnie Rosenthal. The Rocket was one of those lottery-style strikers who would take a wild swing at the ball whenever he was past the halfway line. The majority of balls would end up having to be recovered by vertigo-suffering Charlie the cleaner from the stadium roof on a Saturday evening.

How we lambasted Ronnie. If the Israeli international came on then you knew you were screwed. However, by the end of the evening of March 1st 1995, Spurs fans everywhere had embraced Rosenthal as an honorary legend. The team was trailing 2-0 to Southampton in the FA Cup 5th round replay and just before half-time the Rocket was thrown on.

It was to become one of the best substitutions in Tottenham Hotspur history as the striker scored two goals in two minutes at the very end of the match, forcing the tie into extra time. In the subsequent half-an-hour he completed his hat-trick and the team went on to complete an unlikely 6-2 win. Ronnie's goals were not tap-ins either, they were true rocket shots. Within 45 minutes, a loser was lost and a hero was born.

The Comeback Kings

A similar but not quite as spectacularly reformed character was the lesser known German at White Hart Lane. While Jürgen Klinsmann had been a true legend, Steffen Freund had to work damn hard to achieve his cult status. I was one of those who initially despised the player and his inability to pass forwards. Other clubs' fans hated him for his moaning, fouls and continental flashing of the imaginary card to get a fellow professional booked.

Something happened though to some Spurs fans. The more opposing players and fans hated Steffen, the more some grew to like the guy and realise that he was actually pretty passionate about Spurs. Maybe he didn't have any creative talent but he could stop an opposing attack better than many other midfielders in the Premiership. Soon the boos turned to "shoot" as he searched for but never found a goal in his 141 games for the club. It's no secret that when he left the club we instantly lost our midfield bite.

All of which brings us to the modern crop of Spurs targets who now have to decide which way they are going to go. There were a number who have suffered the sharp edge of fans' tongues last season including Johnnie Jackson, Rohan Ricketts, Noe Pamarot, Thimothee Atouba, Dean Richards and Goran Bunjevcevic. The moans haven't been as bad so far, but they'll come.

We've all got our heroes and our villains and there's no denying that this pantomime is superb entertainment whichever direction it heads in. There are so many players who have felt our anger across the years I've been a supporter and I'm sure that everyone has someone in the current side currently writing their pages in our little black book of irritation.

Thursday October 13th 2005

I CAN PICTURE this morning's scene. Sven calls his children into his office. Becks, Wayne, Little Mikey, Frank and Stevie sit before him, eyes beaming. He sits on the corner of his desk, with his fingers knitted together and his brow furrowed.

He looks at them and says: "Vot are we going do, boys? I can't keep picking you if you're going to get injured and for sure, these others keep coming in and playing better. Silly Stevie, that King boy played a blinder. Now they're all calling for him. All the experts, even that Scottish twat who fancies Carrick."

The door knocks and Jermain Defoe pops his head round. "Not now, you!" shouts the normally calm Swede. Jermain runs off and Sven turns to Michael: "For sure it was lucky you scored, Mikey. I've been trying to keep that boy away from your spot for ages. He doesn't even play anymore." Then both giggle like school kids.

The FA will never admit it, but I bet there was a special team meeting this morning. Is it any coincidence that pretty much every time a new player manages to sneak into Sven's cast-in-stone first eleven and turn the heads of the nation, it's been a Spurs player?

Ledley has actually done it three times. The country's media went wild when he scored in his full debut against Portugal last year; they went crazy for his performance when thrown into the opening game of Euro 2004 against France and this morning the newspapers once again pulled out all the stops with their numerous bad puns on his name.

Jermain Defoe also hit the back of the net on his full debut for England against Poland last year and the headlines were all his the next day. It was the same match that Paul Robinson took on the England gloves from Butterscotch but it wasn't until John Hartson's ginger bonce sent the ball towards his corner that the journalists' fingers began bashing excitedly away. What other recent England goalkeepers have been praised and hailed as much as he was after that game?

Finishing off the quartet is Michael Carrick who, once again with his first senior start, earned the praise and a sackful of love letters from Alan Hansen with his performances in the US of A. That's a heavy Spurs majority with Wright-Phillips and Richardson the only other candidates. Do we put something in the water at the Lane?

Unfortunately, they all have something else in common. Despite their outstanding performances and the fact that they all changed England's play for the better, Mr Eriksson decided that he preferred his unbalanced team of favourites and ditched them soon after. The exception to the rule was Wayne Rooney. Perhaps the retirement of Paul Scholes left a space in Sven's love-in.

However, and this might be a good debate starter, even after all of that you may be surprised to learn that I am not actually a member of the Sack Sven gang. Despite the fact that he has his favourites, shows as much passion as a bag of frozen peas, gives Beckham and Gary Neville far too much power and makes the worst substitutions in the history of substitutions, there's no doubting he's taken England as a team up a level.

He does have flaws but from the depths of Taylor, Wilkinson and Keegan surely we are a better team now. In previous years, I'd fear us being drawn against the likes of Italy, France, Holland, Germany, Argentina and Brazil. With the Swede, I would now only genuinely feel worried if we were matched against the Brazilians, although it would be one hell of a match.

Ode to Jol

Sven's competitive record is still superb, he's taken us easily to major competitions and the match against Germany in Munich and the World Cup game against Argentina proved we can mix it with the best. We used to play a different style of game to the rest of the world which yielded few results, but now we can play them at their game and win.

I'm firmly of the opinion that the whole country should now get behind the team and its bespectacled Swede. Sir Bobby was much maligned before the 1990 World Cup and even told to go home after its early stages by the media. A couple of matches later, we were a Waddle away from glory and the old boy returned a hero. Who's to bet Sven won't do one or two better?

Anyway, I've spent far too much time on England and away from Spurs, so it's back to this weekend and the visit of Everton to the Lane. Am I the only one that thinks the Charlton comeback feels like ages ago? I can scarcely remember the sight of Robbie smashing the ball past Stephan Andersen... oh no wait... yep there it is. Brilliant. What's the score, Bent?

If Ledley can shake off his dead leg then we'll have a pretty strong side and anywhere near a repeat of last season's 5-2 crushing would go down nicely and leave us as the second best team in the country until Monday at least.

Will Robbie's recent Spurs form get him a starting spot or will Jermain's extra freshness and point to prove with his lack of international action see him keep his place? Will Carrick slot straight back in? Will Jenas keep his place or will Reid come back in with Davids back in the middle?

I had hoped to be at the game this weekend and provide a matchday report on my return. However, I was let down by a friend (now been disappeared) who had been promising to buy the tickets since August only to patiently wait until they were sold out before making that important call. With friends like that, who needs Jens Lehmann?

To anyone who is going, I am extremely envious and therefore I expect to hear your voice singing and screaming with your lungs bursting on my radio commentary. Sing for Ledley, sing for Martin but most important of all, sing for our Lilywhites and ensure those Toffeemen stick even longer to the bottom of the Premiership.

Saturday 15th October 2005

FA Premiership
Tottenham Hotspur 2 Everton 0
Attendance – 36,267
Spurs goalscorers: Mido, Jenas

Tuesday 18th October 2005

HAVE SPURS MANAGED to crack something that held the team back last season, robbing us of vital points against smaller teams who stood camped in an army of nine in their own half?

The last three matches have produced nine points and some fine results against teams who packed the midfield with five players. Darren Bent and his namesake Marcus ploughed a lone furrow up front for their sides, while Brian McBride watched in frustration as sometime partners Luis Boa Morte and Tomasz Radzinski fell back on the wings of the Fulham midfield.

Last season we threw points down the drain against midfield-heavy sides such as Bolton x2, Charlton x2, Norwich, West Brom x2 and Crystal Palace x2. I'm not sure what's more irritating, that we missed so many opportunities to beat the three promoted sides or that apart from the Canaries we failed to learn any lessons from each first encounter.

So what's the difference this year? One man who didn't start any of the above nine games was Hossam Ahmed Mido. For the most part, the partnership up front in those matches was the Smurfs duo, Robbie and Jermain. Fredi Kanoute played a part in some of the games to varying degrees of success.

Having spent the summer staring in horror at Andy Reid in the Spurs Lodge canteen, Mido came back a changed man. He gave his secret stash of Mars bars to the excited little Irishman and hit the gym and training pitches. True to his promise to big Martin, or 'Papa Smurf' as Robbie and Jermain call him, the Egyptian returned to action in the Peace Cup a mere shadow of his chunky former self.

His heading ability is right up there among the best in Europe and has been lauded by coaches in Holland, France and Italy. Jol hardly utters a sentence nowadays that doesn't contain "Mido", "Shpecial", "fantashtic" or "head". Playing against a team with five across the middle, Spurs have been able this campaign to bypass the open-mouthed midfielders with a ball from Robbo or a defender over the top onto the head of the tall Alice-banded striker.

Don't get me wrong, Fredi was terrific in the air, especially with his Velcro chest hair, but he didn't put himself about as much as his successor. Can you honestly see the Malian leaping wholeheartedly into a headed challenge in the lashing rain? For Mido it's all part of the fun and he'll keep doing it until the final whistle or a red card is produced by Rob Styles.

Is it any coincidence that we didn't pick up any

wins in Mido's three-game suspended absence? His partnership with Defoe is growing with each game as is his confidence as a talisman within the Spurs team. His goal and flick to begin the move for the second on Saturday were both sublime. Against Charlton, he glanced the ball on for Ledley's goal and notched one himself before playing a vital role in distracting the opposition by lying prostrate on the ground for the winner.

I wouldn't be surprised if Martin Jol is currently in Italy holding Roma manager Luciano Spalletti in a headlock, making him an offer he can't refuse. Something like: "Give ush the boy or I'll put my fisht through your faysh." Such is the importance of the new Pharaoh of the Lane.

Another sight on Saturday could prove to be a second bow to our arrow against defensively minded teams. Jermaine Jenas' break from midfield into the box to head the second goal was a sign to other clubs why the youngster was signed. As Jol is aware and is probably working on daily, the goldfish bowl-hater has the pace and skill to be a fine Paul Scholes-esque poacher.

Jol's face when the header went in spoke volumes and if Jenas can build on that moment then his timed runs will throw teams' tactics out of the window. It certainly whipped up the crowd. It reminded me of Poyet in his pomp. The beauty of cracking a defensive team is that once you steal that advantage they have no choice but to abandon their plans. Then the real Spurs can destroy them.

In the absence of Jenas, it seems Tainio is being groomed by the giant Dutchman for a similar role as he proved against Charlton with his fine runs and passing. It will also help the team's cause that Edgar Davids' tenacity and harrying is probably equal to two opposition midfielders. Is anyone else looking forward as much as me to him squashing Alan Smith, Cesc Fabregas and Mathieu Flamini?

It's going to be one hell of a test on Saturday against the Red Devils, but it was heartening to see them stutter against Lille without Wayne Rooney. Although he will return at Old Trafford at the weekend, if you can keep him under wraps for as long as possible you stand a chance against the rest as Milenko and his mates proved tonight.

It's certainly a different team that's heading up to Manchester from the one that participated on the night when Pedro did what Pele couldn't. As well as Edgar Davids chomping away in the middle, whoever plays at left-back for them will have to deal with Aaron "watch my heels" Lennon. Then there's Mido partnering someone up front rather than Robbie Keane battling alone for scraps.

Rio Ferdinand was unconvincing again tonight and I look forward to seeing him being really troubled by our confident players on Saturday. Both the matches last season were tight affairs but with their defensive lapses in recent games and our improving side, could this be the start of something special?

A win or even a well-earned point at Old Trafford would set us up nicely for a certain meeting with some mid-table side next week. So come on big Martin, get the boys whipped up and ready and let's give Sir Alex a nightmare in the Theatre of Dreams.

Saturday 22nd October 2005

FA Premiership
Manchester United 1 Tottenham Hotspur 1
Attendance – 67,856
Spurs goalscorer: Jenas

Sunday 23rd October 2005

THE COCKEREL ON the top of White Hart Lane had his head bowed in sadness today as it was exactly a year since the man who made Tottenham Hotspur passed away. The term 'legend' is bandied about nowadays but Bill Nicholson was one of those elite few that the term was originally intended for.

It's difficult to overstate what the 85-year-old was to the club. Had it not been for his glory, glory years the name Tottenham Hotspur would not reverberate around the world as it does today. The style and attractive play that is synonymous with Spurs, our European and league history-making feats, would have probably been found elsewhere in the country.

He was Mr Tottenham Hotspur. He made his debut as a player in 1938 when the club had very little to its name. He was part of Arthur Rowe's 'Push and Run' side which brought the club its first championship in 1951. Three years after Rowe's departure, Bill took the reins and dragged the Lilywhites onto the world stage.

Within another three years, in 1961, his stylish and talented side became the first team in England to complete the double since Preston North End did it in 1889, the league's first season. In 1963, Spurs became the first British side to capture a European trophy, bringing home the Cup Winners' Cup. During his time, we were the first English team to win the League Cup twice and to play in three major European finals.

These are records that will stand forever, stitched into the fabric of football. However great other sides may consider themselves now or in the future, Spurs fans can be safe in the knowledge that Bill did it first and with style.

It was all about the style and the entertainment. He once said: "We must always consider our supporters, for without them there would be no professional football. It would be better to have more fans watching football the way they like it played, rather than have a few fans watching football the way we would like it played."

When the dreaming of Tottenham fans is called into question, it should be answered with probably the great man's most famous quote: "It is better to fail aiming high than to succeed aiming low. And we of Spurs have set our sights very high, so high in fact that even failure will have in it an echo of glory."

If a player was not committed to the Tottenham Hotspur cause they were surplus to requirements. The man who should have been knighted had the club coursing through his veins. His blood was undoubtedly white and navy, never red.

It's a testament to his legacy that the younger fans like myself can eulogise his years of success as well as the older ones who were lucky enough to see it happen before their eyes. As wonderful as the videos and books make those marvellous nights of football seem, I can only dream how it must have felt to watch some of that football being played. It makes my skin tingle. The man is gone but his presence will always be felt. Every time the words Tottenham Hotspur are spoken from North London to Paris, from Madrid to Tokyo and from New York to Cape Town it will be because of Bill Nicholson. Thanks for it all, 'Sir' Bill, we owe you everything.

Saturday October 29th 2005

FA Premiership
Tottenham Hotspur 1 Arsenal 1
Attendance – 36,154
Spurs goalscorer: King

The Comeback Kings

WHAT A DIFFERENCE a year or even a week makes. Last Saturday night I was walking around with a smile on my face content with a point and a fantastic free kick. Tonight, I can't stop thinking of what might have been.

In the ensuing hours, results have gone Spurs' way as those below slipped up, except for the gravity-defying Wigan who swapped places with Charlton after their last-gasp win. Now, as I flick over the channel, Manchester United have just toppled over at the Riverside.

So we have kept our third place, but I can't help but feel we should be sitting pretty in second now. In that first half today, any newcomer at White Hart Lane would surely have turned to the person next to him and said: "So the team in white usually win, do they?"

We were rampant in those 45 minutes. In the crowd, we were singing and screaming at the top of our voices. We were on top against the enemy and they couldn't touch us. Michael Carrick gave every midfielder on the park a lesson in pulling the strings. Campbell and Toure struggled to contain Defoe and Mido while Gael Clichy looked like he'd had a messy accident every time Aaron Lennon picked up the ball.

Tainio slotted perfectly into the Davids role and the back four were in control. We looked like scoring every time we went forward and were dangerous from each set piece as The King soon proved. Even Carrick shocked everyone by taking a chance with a long-range effort.

However, that old cliché (not Gael) is as true as it is painful – you have to take your chances. With each near miss or block from the whinging German, the possibility of the Goons getting back into the game increased just a little. Actually, as we are on the subject of the calamitous

Ode to Jol

Lehmann, have you ever seen a more pathetic example of a professional sportsman?

I have never seen a goalkeeper fall to the floor, writhing in agony like a tripped schoolgirl in a playground, as often as Jenny does when a player invades his personal space. Jermain Defoe got booked for simply walking near him. How that buffoon can argue that he should be his nation's trusted guardian, I'll never know.

A special word for Judas as well. The expected boos seemed to really get to him this time. An early misplaced pass belied his calm exterior and my heart skipped a beat at one point as I thought the moment we'd all been waiting for had arrived – a Judas own goal at White Hart Lane. It sliced wide for a corner but for a split second my head was full of glorious newspaper headlines and images.

I loved the fact that after Campbell left Tainio on the floor covered in blood with that cowardly elbow, Jol seemed to be on the sidelines saying to the Finn: "What? That ashhole elbowed you? I'm gonna kill 'im!" He raised himself up to his full height, ran to the white line and started yelling at Judas, the ref and anyone that would listen. If he could have replaced Tainio with himself, he would have. What a sight that first challenge would have been.

However, after 45 minutes of free-flowing positive football came a murderous half-time. Normally that special 15 minutes when the giant Dutchman slams players' heads together and tells them to "sshape up or sship out" before they emerge with steel in their eyes. Instead I got the feeling today that that was happening across the tunnel while the Spurs boys were sitting back smoking Martin's cigars and clinking whisky glasses, toasting their success.

Carrick's influence shrunk as quickly as a Spurs shirt

after one of my wife's washes and we let them run the majority of the play. They didn't exactly threaten a lot but we just kept giving the ball to them at every opportunity. Mido started to tire up front and we weren't winning the ball and holding it up.

The only man who really kept going in attack was Jermain Defoe, who I thought had a really selfless hard-working game. His fantastic dribble into the area deserved so much more than a limp Lehmann wrist. He was kicked and crashed into but kept holding onto the ball, whipping crosses in and bringing others into the play. He's not scoring at the moment but his all-round game has come on in leaps and bounds.

Then came Robbo's head-in-hands moment. England's Number One has saved us on more occasions than humanly possible and pulled off some more great saves today. How unfortunate for the big guy that the only two mistakes he's made in the past two years have come in two of our biggest games of the season. I did notice that he was struggling with the sun in the moments before the goal and was constantly shielding his eyes.

I'm not sure if he needed to come out for the cross, especially if he was affected by the light, but of all the people to present the goal on a plate to – oh God, not the most annoying Frenchman in the Premiership. The guy hasn't even got the strength to knock a ball off of a penalty spot but we let him score against us. I have never screamed so loud in pain and anguish as I did when it went over the line. One bloke a couple of seats away from me looked genuinely scared, as if I was transforming into a werewolf.

It was a disappointing point at the end of the day but I guess that's a measure of how far we've come. A year ago we didn't even get that but this time around people expected us to win, most of all ourselves and on the balance of play and chances we deserved it and should have done it. Hearing Whinger on the radio after the match, he certainly feels it was a bit of a victory for them.

On the plus side though, Liverpool, Manchester United and Arsenal – supposedly in the big four – have not been able to beat us and we could have won all three matches. Our expectations have been raised from their already ridiculously high levels but we're sitting third in the league, in a comfy Champions League spot, and have a run of games coming up that takes in all three promoted sides.

We've proved we can match the big boys in the first quarter of the season, so now it's time to discard that age-old Tottenham problem of stuttering against the teams we are supposed to beat. Jol has eight days to prepare the troops, make sure they take confidence from the last two games, and put some Wanderers to the sword.

Chapter Five

November
Win, Lose and Draw

Monday November 7th 2005

FA Premiership
Bolton Wanderers 1 Tottenham Hotspur 0
Attendance – 26,634

Tuesday November 8th 2005

I DON'T KNOW which was more painful – the sight of Paul Stalteri's long and billowing cross thudding against the crossbar in the final seconds of last night's match or the fact that in the resulting frustration I jammed a pen into my sofa. Failing to remember I had the offending device in my hand was the last thing on my mind, at least until the wife began strangling me. For once again, Spurs had come into a match that had been proclaimed as a "real test for this young side". The result will confirm that we failed but the truth was that we matched them in every area but the all-important scoreline.

Tottenham arrived at the Reebok Stadium with the only unbeaten away record left in the Premiership and the mysterious absence of Aaron – rumours were floating that he had returned to the Chocolate Factory.

The Jolly Orange Giant set out his stall with Teemu Tainio and Edgar Davids providing the midfield muscle to compliment Carrick and Jenas' guile.

Ode to Jol

Therefore he must have been delighted when his team found themselves penned in their own penalty area for the first nine minutes of the match. It didn't help that every time El-Hadji Diouf picked up the ball, his glass ankles shattered and he fell to the floor, with spit flying everywhere. Out of interest, did anyone else notice that after one particular dive, he gave the biggest possible toothy smirk to the referee as if to say: "You fell for that one, matey, didn't you?"

After much battling and clearing of the lines, Spurs finally managed a decent breakaway when the linesman made the first of his "extremely professional" decisions. Despite standing exactly in line with Jermain Defoe and the defensive line, the assistant decided that one of the diminutive striker's boot laces was slightly offside.

The admittedly impressive Kevin Nolan then scored one of those goals you can't really complain about. Perhaps some will argue that Diouf had handled the ball in the air but we would have deemed it harsh at the other end, and there was no doubting the quality of the rocket finish from outside the area.

What was so infuriating was that within 60 seconds we had the ball in their net after yet more good play from the quick-thinking Tainio. But once again that slow, ponderous yellow flag was raised high and Defoe was ruled offside for no apparent reason. A Specsavers advert on the linesman's arm would have been more appropriate than the Gooner-loving Fly Emirates badges.

After a worrying Nolan shot against the post and a possibly more worrying show of Lee Young-Pyo's left-foot strength in front of the gaping Bolton goal, we went into the break having allowed the home side only one shot on target, albeit a goal-scoring one.

In the second half we were far the better team, perhaps because Kevin Davies, the fulcrum of much of their attacking play, had left the field with an injury. Mido, who didn't have one of his better games, could have still produced something special when he beat three of their defenders before his goalbound shot was blocked by the other seven diving Bolton defenders.

Jenas was finally starting to get forward and his late scissor-kick deserved so much more as did Mido's post-hitting follow-up. Davids showed that he is definitely the difference in Spurs' away form compared to last season as he harried and hassled everyone in a white shirt. He is still wasted on the left side and we could do with him driving through the middle, leaving opponents falling in his wake, rather than tracking wingers.

Defoe had another impressive game without reward. He covered more ground than most players on the pitch and when the going got tough, he was among the tackles in Tottenham's half. Dawson and Stalteri had good games as did King apart from a few rare moments of overconfidence. On our captain's 'stamp' in Stelios' face, surely he was trying to get a foot on the ground to push off. He wasn't even looking at the midfielder and I think the Bolton fans realised this as they gave up on booing after a few minutes.

Then that damn lick of paint took away the prospect of another two weeks in third place. We had thrown everything at them in that second half. I even saw Martin Jol emerge from the dugout at one point holding an enormous kitchen sink aloft. However, the night was to end in despair and a damaged sofa.

Is it better to be bellowing at the moon in anguish after a poor performance or one where you have given everything and just fallen short? Mark Lawrenson didn't believe that our 'fancy-dans' would be up for the fight on a cold and windy night in Bolton. With a battling and bruising performance from all quarters on that blustery evening, we proved him wrong in spirit if not in result.

The chance to recover is at hand with four games against teams we should beat, "should" being the important word. We take on all of the promoted sides and Portsmouth, with three of the matches at White Hart Lane.

After reasonable results from a tricky run of games, we now have to make sure we put these 'lesser' teams to the Lilywhite sword. If we do then, in four games' time, last night's result could be a distant memory and even Lawro may raise his eyebrows at least once.

Sunday November 13th 2005

TODAY I TOOK the liberty of drugging the White Hart Lane tea lady, Mavis, and taking her place. Dressed in an absurdly small flowery apron, I was eventually rumbled by security guards but before they could drag me out of Martin Jol's office, I managed to grab hold of his diary. Fools! Here is last Monday's entry; try doing it in Martin's voice...

Monday November 8th 2005

5.30am

I GOT UP eshpecially early today to finish last night's leftovers and talk to my brother Cock and my nephew Dick back in Holland. They like to get me up on matchday mornings. We put our heads together and I think we have a shtrategy for beating Bolton today. I kiss my varioush managerial awards and then my wife and as I'm feeling shtrong today I decide to walk from my apartment to White Hart Lane.

8.25am

HAVE JUST DROPPED off a gang of muggers at the police station. I caught them trying to rob an old lady along Sheven Shisters Road. Naughty boys. I threw them in the shell and have a chuckle with some nice policemen and make them feel better about their job.

9.00am

I FINALLY ARRIVE at the shtadium. There is a shtrange man shtanding on the corner. He is all alone and is shtaring at me and this book as I write in it. He's the one who keeps shouting up at Mr Levy's office. Shomething Gold, I think hish name ish. I don't like him, he looks like he's planning something and keeps shtaring at my journal. I shcowl at him and he shcrurries around the corner.

9.30am

AFTER SHAYING GOOD morning to everyone in the building I walk into my office. I open my cupboard and hand my jacket to Johnnie Jackson who takes it inside and shmiles. Nice boy. I plop down at my desk and type my password into the computer... I8ARSENAL. Up comes my background picture of Bill Nick. He is a beautiful man. One day I will be just like him. After shending shome abushive emails to Whinger down the road to make me happy, I shettle down to shee what the media boys have written about me. As usual, it's all good and I feel a million euros. Then Mr Comolli walks in.

11.00am

I AM NOT very happy now at all. Mr Comolli said that we could not sign Ronaldo from Madrid. I felt very mad and I asked if it would help if I crushed someone at Real. Mr Comolli tells me that I can maybe do that next week if he still can't get the boy. After the boss walked out I was still very angry and I opened one of my drawers and took out my shtress relief toy. Little Wayne's head was badly shquashed after I had finished.

2.10pm

MY BOYS HAVE just finished eating their lunch. I just saw Jermain in the corridor and I gave him a big hug and told him we will be winners tonight. He went very red and I realised I was hurting him. When I put him down he ran off. Shilly boy.

7.55pm

I GIVE A very shexy team talk and all the boys go out the dressing room with their heads up high. Chrissy is in tears and tells me it was beautiful. As I pass Jermain in the tunnel, I shcoop him up and tell him to express himshelf out there. He gets all embarrassed in front of the Bolton lads and tries to wriggle down but I know he really loves me.

10.15pm

BLOODY HELL AND a clog full of bollocks. Those shwines bloody won and we had a perfectly good goal ruled offshide. I was sho shocked by their shecond goal that I threw little Aaron into the shtands. One of the physios shouted at me and told me I could have injured him. I flung him at Sam Allardyce at the final whistle. I don't like looshing.

11.55pm

I SHQUEEZED LITTLE Wayne through the whole tape of the game and my wife had to take him to hoshpital. But I am happy again now. Mr Comolli just rang. He told me that he had agreed terms with a boy called Fernando in Shpain and that Downing lad from Middlesbrough. We will both introduce them to everybody on February 1st. I am sho happy I could shing. I must go now as I can hear my wife coming in the door and I am feeling like giving her shome big man loving. Goodnight diary.

Sunday November 20th 2005

FA Premiership
Tottenham Hotspur 1 West Ham United 1
Attendance – 36,154
Spurs goalscorer: Mido

ONCE AGAIN THREE points slipped away from Spurs' grasp because the team just does not have that killer instinct. Was I the only one who felt that as each minute passed without a second goal, the likelihood grew that we would pay the price?

The irony is that now the media has picked Tottenham Hotspur among its dark horses and acknowledged the progress made on the white side of North London, gone are the 5-1s and 5-2s of last season.

In their place this campaign has been a bunch of solid results. No thrashings for or against, instead a whole bunch of single or double goal winning margins. There is undoubtedly a feeling of strength to the team now but very little in the way of killer instinct or defence-splitting final ball.

West Ham did not deserve a point today – whatever Alan Pardew thinks and whatever big Martin says to cover up another sorry display of finishing and chance creating. We dominated the game in all but the final third and the chances we did have were poorly taken. Mido, Defoe and Jenas all had excellent chances in the final couple of minutes to wrap the game up but all went wide or softly into Shaka Hislop's hands.

The truth is, however, that the game should have been wrapped up by the 60–65 minute mark. Martin Jol gave Robbie Keane the chance today to prove his starting place in a game that I thought would have been ripe for Jermain Defoe to grab a couple.

I'm all for swapping strikers when they aren't performing but Defoe had played well in his last couple of games and surely he would have been fired up following yet another Sven snub and the prospect of silencing the Hammers' boo boys.

Keane played well enough today, but I just don't think he had the direct, pacey attacking skills that Defoe would have brought to the scene. Next week or last week would have been the ideal time to start the Irishman, a man who knows how you often score against your old sides at White Hart Lane.

The difference between mid-table obscurity and breaking into the upper echelons is the ability to be ruthless and put teams to the sword. I have still to be convinced this season that our youngsters have that mentality drilled into them yet. For instance, while Mido's heading ability is among the best in the league, his shooting from the edges of the area is shocking, as Paul Robinson admitted this month in one interview where he touched on the Egyptian's practice sessions.

While we've proved this season that we have the character to come back into matches, we had enough reasonable chances today to bury West Ham in front of the White Hart Lane faithful. Dustmen around Tottenham will still be finding balls next week walloped over by the flying boots of Lee Young-Pyo – and that was with his right foot.

Win, Lose and Draw

I dismissed notions early on that we had purchased a left-back with no left foot but I'm starting to creep towards that line of thinking myself as each game passes. He did have a decent game but the day he puts in a good cross or shot with his left foot will be only minutes after Carrick puts the ball into the opposition net.

Don't get me wrong, he's an excellent player who is always looking to link up play but I get the feeling he's a right-back who was told to play on the left when he was young to fill a gap and got stuck there.

We are in this run of matches now where we must pick up points if we are to stay in the European places or thereabouts. If we continue this recent trend of throwing away leads then worry will start to spread through the team. We'll never be comfortable with a single goal advantage and those playing against us will know that. If we'd put away chances against the Goons and today, we'd be sitting in second place right now.

There will always be controversial decisions, what with the disallowed goal against Bolton, the foul that led to Arsenal's goal-scoring free kick and today's equaliser well after the added time had finished. The fact remains though that Spurs should not have to moan about these sorts of decisions as they shouldn't be the be-all and end-all of our matches. Games should be sewn up without the need for refereeing assistance.

I hope that Clive Allen is told to take a few days' holiday from the reserves this week and take a few extra striking sessions with all of our strikers, midfielders and a certain South Korean left-back. It's all very well to produce beautiful concise football in your own half and just inside the opponents' but we need our players to be bombing into the area from all angles, finishing off moves from all over the place.

There have often been times in recent games when

the ball is whipped into a box containing Mido and four opposition defenders with our midfielders waiting around the edges looking for rebounds and scraps rather than throwing themselves at the ball. Jenas proved in his first few matches that defenders struggle to pick up those runs. That perfect final ball to the forward is also something that is proving too rare in this run of games.

I'm going to dip my head out of the Spurs world for a few days and let the anger subside. My sofa is still suffering from the stabbing incident of two weeks ago and today I came very close to strangling a fellow supporter who was whining particularly loudly next to me after the goal. I will return however next Saturday with renewed vigour and the hope that my Lilywhites will return to ruthless ways.

Saturday November 26th 2005

FA Premiership
Wigan Athletic 1 Tottenham Hotspur 2
Attendance – 22,611
Spurs goalscorers: Keane, Davids

Tuesday November 29th 2005

SATURDAY SAW MARTIN Jol's 50th game in charge of Tottenham Hotspur. Although now the most recognised face in Tottenham, when the big Dutchman arrived in the summer of 2004, it was as the lowest-profile edge of a revolutionary Spurs triangle.

There had been heavy talk from many media outlets that a deal had been done for a highly-rated assistant coach to join from Holland.

Eventually the fans got their glimpse of Jol, an 8ft 3ins giant, who had been bandied around the papers and internet as the final link of the Santini/Arnesen 'Dream Team'.

He had spent a couple of seasons as a player in England at Coventry and West Bromwich Albion, even scoring against the Lilywhites for the latter. His most notable claim to fame in the eyes of English football fans was that he was reported to have been in the frame as Fergie's right-hand man at Old Trafford before the grumpy Scot's Portugeezer returned.

It was rumoured then that he was turned down by the Knight of Manchester due to having munched through Holland's supply of Edam. However, there was no confirmation of that spurious gossip apart from a small quote from one 'cheese expert' from Rotterdam. Fergie later confirmed the discussions with the man with the big reputation, but said the only reason the tactician did not end up in Manchester was that his Portuguese pal wanted to come back.

What Spurs got was a tough-looking, articulate coach with a top reputation in his homeland. His current look-alike among the Lilywhite faithful is the television gangster Tony Soprano. As a player he certainly took no prisoners and was a fearsome midfielder whose bite was as bad as his bark. He was a Dutch international and was named as the country's player of the year in 1987. He played for ADO Den Haag, Bayern Munich and Twente before being signed as Bryan Robson's replacement in the centre of the park at West Bromwich Albion. At the Hawthorns, he reached the semi-finals of both the FA Cup and the League Cup.

He spent a season with Coventry City before returning to Holland to see out his playing career with his first club, Den Haag. After hanging up his boots, the Dutch side took him on as their head coach. Den Haag were languishing in the Dutch third division – the Hoofdklasse – which is an amateur league. He took the club up the divisions with two promotions in three years. He then moved onto another semi-professional side, Scheveningen, who he led to the Dutch non-league championship title in his first and only year there.

The professional clubs circled and he was soon snapped up by Roda JC. Much to their delight, his work in the lower league was no fluke. With the then slightly more hairy Jol at the helm, the Eredivisie club captured the Dutch Cup – the FA Cup of the Netherlands. It was their first trophy in 30 years.

After a couple of seasons, he took on a challenge that would test all his motivational and tactical acumen. He was installed as head coach at RKC Waalwijk, a struggling outfit in the top Dutch league – think Wigan without the finances or stadium. Like Achilles striding through the Achaean army, Jol dragged the team up the table until they became regular challengers for the European qualification spots. He earned himself a reputation for developing promising young players in a team that played attractive football.

His remarkable achievement with such a shoestring budget did not go unnoticed. He was named the Dutch Football Writers' Coach of the year in 2001, and the following season picked up the Dutch players' and coaches' Coach of the Year award. When PSV Eindhoven's Frank Arnesen was appointed Tottenham Hotspur's new sporting director he firmly set Jol in his sights as a travel companion.

There were early rumours that it was the Dane's wish for Jol to be installed as Spurs head coach. However, after almost a year of David Pleat, Lilywhite fans were drooling in desperation for a big name. Enter stage right France manager Jacques Santini – complete with the English language skills of a hamster and

Leicester's Mark De Vries scores the second most embarrassing goal of the season.

Robbie Keane scores one of the best goals of Spurs' season against Blackburn.

Mido wheels away after scoring the winning goal against Blackburn.

Robbo acknowledges the Tottenham faithful at St Andrews.

West Brom keeper Tomasz Kuszczak gifts Spurs with a late penalty at the Lane.

Michael Dawson receives his marching orders against Newcastle United.

Michael Carrick fires past David James to condemn Manchester City to defeat.

Robbie Keane's goal bids the perfect farewell to Highbury.

the attacking flair of Tony Adams. Jol decided that although it was a step down position-wise, the role of assistant manager at Spurs was most definitely a step up in terms of his career.

On his arrival he told the fans: "With players like Ossie Ardiles and Glenn Hoddle, Spurs have always played beautiful football. The club has a glorious history." His direct, passionate views became the main voice on the club's official website as Santini worked on his English. The players, in their quotes, were always quick to compliment the man-management and tactical skills of the assistant manager, sometimes at the expense of Santini's influence.

Despite the players' bond with Jol, few would have expected Santini to leave the club within only four months. His replacement, however, could not have been more obvious. The fans, who had been won over by the words and tales of Jol, were united in their wish for him to take control. The players told Arnesen the Jolly Oranje Giant was their pick for the job.

It is legend among fans that as the board were considering his appointment, Martin Jol marched into their conference room and delivered an impassioned speech. He wore his Spurs blazer with the cockerel over his heart. He touched the badge throughout as he stood before the open-mouthed businessmen, laying his passion and credentials on the table for all to see.

He eulogised about the club's grand and glittering history and let the members know in no uncertain terms that he was the man to bring those days back. Well aware of the 'knight' behind the history, he spoke of his burning desire to become the Bill Nicholson of the current generation of Lilywhites. It was the interview to beat all interviews and, if the tale is to be believed, the board recommended his installation as head coach with immediate effect.

The decision and the continuity it brought would prove to be extremely wise. Unlike Santini, Jol was used to the continental system with another person running the transfers and contracts side of things. He was free to develop players and drum in his tactics. It was not long before "He's got no hair, but we don't care... Martin Jol", began to resound around White Hart Lane. He brought flowing football back to the North London club and after only a month in charge he won the Premiership Manager of the Month award.

Unlike previous Spurs managers, he also became a darling of the British media. Here was a coach who spoke his mind with honesty, respect and a healthy dollop of humour – a journalist's dream. Jol swiftly restored Tottenham's reputation on and off the pitch. His homeland was watching with interest and the big guns at Ajax looked on with envious eyes, making it known they were willing to offer the Dutchman the biggest job in Holland.

Jol came straight out and might as well have been wearing a Spurs scarf around his neck as he told reporters: "If you want a clear answer, I will give it. I am not interested in the Ajax job at all. Tottenham is a challenge for me. They are a good club and are looking after me. The fans are terrific. I am happy here and committed to the club."

He was true to his word and signed a new three-year deal in the summer – not before he took a revitalised side back up the table into ninth place, only three points off a spot in Europe. The last game of the season at home to Blackburn saw the Dutch master receive a standing ovation from the stadium as he led his players around the ground.

Hope had returned to Tottenham Hotspur and,

working with Daniel Levy, the summer saw Jol welcome fresh young English faces in Jermaine Jenas, Aaron Lennon, Wayne Routledge and Tom Huddlestone as well as the experience of Edgar Davids, Lee Young-Pyo, Paul Stalteri and Teemu Tainio. Relics of the previous regimes like Fredi Kanoute, Erik Edman, Simon Davies and Thimothee Atouba were discarded for decent fees. Martin Jol had stamped his mark on the club.

The season thus far has only strengthened his imprint on the club. His half-century victory against Wigan means the team has racked up six wins, six draws and a mere two losses. He has the full support of the fans and the players and will undoubtedly be celebrating many more anniversaries at Tottenham Hotspur.

Chapter Six

December
Even Carrick Scored

Saturday December 3rd 2005

FA Premiership
Tottenham Hotspur 3 Sunderland 2
Attendance – 36,244
Spurs goalscorers: Mido, Keane, Carrick

Sunday December 4th 2005

THE LETTER ARRIVED on Thursday from the mysterious Mr H Goddle. He explained briefly that he was a disgruntled ex-employee of Tottenham Hotspur and wanted me to see what really went on at the club. Paper-clipped to the letter were extensive blueprints of Spurs Lodge.

So I waited until I had the cover of darkness and made my way by bus to the training ground in Chigwell. Hiding in nearby bushes until I was sure the coast was clear, I emerged in my commando gear – to others the Spurs home goalie shirt, a pair of tracksuit trousers and a black bobble hat. Unfolding Mr Goddle's plans from my backpack I followed them closely and managed to sneak into a ventilation shaft on the side of the lodge.

Once holed up inside I munched on my home-made fish paste sandwiches before settling down for the night. When the first light flickered on Friday morning, I opened my journal. What follows is my diary of that day.

9.00am

I HAVE WRIGGLED into position above Martin Jol's office and the big man has just walked in with Damien Comolli and two other men... Here is what they have just said:

MJ: Theesh are my brudders, Cock and Dick, Mr Comolli. I am sho happy we can get them on board. They have lotsh of exshperiensh as coaches and referees.

DC: Zis iz no problem, Martin. Have you any thoughts on where they should scout or would you like me to assign them?

MJ: Pershonally, I would love to shee Cock all over Holland because that ish where we are from and we know it well. Ash for my other brother here, well if poshible we should start using our Dick in Spain this weekend... What's sho funny? Why are you giggling? Wait, wait come back.

9.45am

IT HAS BEEN quiet for a while since the big man chased the sniggering Frenchman down the hall. So I have moved to a grate above the reception area where Sean Davis works behind the desk, fielding calls. Someone's coming... Edgar Davids has just walked in with Aaron Lennon sitting on his shoulders eating an ice cream.

Pedro Mendes is just behind wearing a hairnet. Grzegorz Rasiak has been stopped and is being searched at the entrance by Noe Pamarot the door guard, who doesn't know "who ze hell he is".

10.00am

THERE'S A TEAM meeting going on in one of the rooms. I can see all the players except Michael Carrick, who walks in after everyone else. Big Martin tells him there's a spare seat at the front but the midfielder replies that he prefers to stay at the back and stands just in front of Michael Dawson and Ledley King, much to their annoyance.

10.15am

I HAVE FOUND the changing rooms and all the stars are switching from their expensive suits into their training gear. On one side Jermaine Jenas hangs his Armani jacket on a hanger, opens his locker and hands it to Rodrigo Defendi who is nestled inside. The door is closed once again on the excellently-named young Brazilian.

10.30am

IT'S ALL GONE quiet at the moment as most of the players are now on the training pitches. However, I have made friends with a small rat whose face looks surprisingly like Bob Dowie's. After I share my Pepperami with him, we debate whether Crystal Palace will ever make it back to the Premiership. Little Bob talks a good game and I soon concede defeat.

11.00am

AFTER A BIT of a wander, I discover a small room with a blackboard on the wall. Jermain Defoe is frantically scribbling what looks like lines on it with a piece of chalk. I really have to press my face against the grill and squint to see what he is scrawling... Now I can see.

He has written over and over again: "All offsides and no goals make Jermain a dull boy." My watch scrapes against the shaft and he suddenly looks up with wild eyes, I scramble back into the safety of the darkness and after a while he returns to his scribbling.

12.00am

NOTHING MUCH TO report as I guess the players are still going through the motions outside in the sunshine. The only thing of note I have seen in the last hour has been Goran Bunjevcevic mopping a few of the hallway floors. Judging by the number of fringe players working in odd jobs around the lodge, I guess Daniel Levy wasn't kidding when he said there won't be a January sale in the transfer window.

12.30pm

I AM AWOKEN from an afternoon nap by a light coming from one nearby grill, illuminating the tunnel. I crawl on my belly over to the source just as the light fades. It's the treatment room. Pedro Mendes is there with an older woman I assume is Dr Charlotte. Wayne Routledge jumps up from a treatment table and jogs out. The door suddenly bursts open and physios bring a screaming Teemu Tainio in and place him on the table. I wince as I realise he has a broken leg.

Pedro bends over and places a palm on the Finn's head to comfort him. Then he moves his hands to the horribly fractured limb. I am blinded suddenly by a beam of light which floods the shaft. By the time my eyes adjust again, Tainio is standing hugging the Portugeezer. I suppose this is why Spurs aren't considered the sicknotes anymore. Pedro looks up directly at me, smiles and walks out of the room.

1.00pm

IT'S LUNCH TIME and I have manoeuvred above the canteen. The wonderful smells are making me really hungry. Behind the counter, Michael Brown is serving up all kinds of delicious food.

I can see all the players are tucking in but I do feel sorry for poor little Lee-Young Pyo. Andy Reid is sitting to the Korean's left and keeps pulling the defender's plate of chicken nuggets towards him. For some reason, Derek 'Lee' Zoolander can't use his left side and keeps turning to his right while the stocky Irishman swipes all the food.

Ode to Jol

2.00pm

AFTER FEASTING ON a Dairylea Dunker with my mate Bob, who had returned wearing a tiny Palace shirt, I have pressed on along the ventilation system and to my joy have found a grill which looks out onto the training pitches.

My joy quickly changes to shock as I realise there is not a ball to be seen – just pandemonium. Players are running here, there and everywhere chased by something I can't see. Every so often a red dot appears on one of their foreheads and they run off the pitch screaming. Martin Jol is bellowing with laughter on the sidelines.

After ten minutes, with players collapsed by the sides struggling for breath, Robbie Keane stands alone in the centre circle. Suddenly Edgar appears from nowhere with his dreadlocks flowing, wearing what looks like metal armour over parts of his body. He emits a mighty bellow and the two begin to trade blows.

Edgar eventually wins and the Irishman walks off the pitch red-faced. Is this the new winning mentality Jol and Davids have instilled? On a side-note I can see a journalist in the bushes scribbling down notes. Must remember to check the papers at the weekend to see if the story has been broken.

3.00pm

I THINK THERE is someone in here with me. My suspicions have been growing for the past half an hour. I keep hearing what sounds like an enormous pair of thighs rubbing against metal every so often and then the word "murd". Even my rat-faced friend has long since run off leaving a small note saying: "I have all I need, thanks."

Wait... something is very close... My leg!...aaaarrgh!!! I bet you're wondering how I managed to write down aaaarrgh, aren't you? Well I'm a quick... aaaarrgh!

8.00pm

I AM BACK home now after a bit of a stop-off at Chigwell Police Station on the High Road. That kind Mr Goddle bailed me out through a representative who looked a hell of a lot like John Gorman. I had to photocopy this diary at the station for him, which he said he would pass onto my mysterious saviour.

As you can probably guess, Noe was the one who tracked me down in the ventilation system. He crushed me with his thighs like that Bond woman and flung me down into the reception area below. I landed on Sean Davis so don't expect to see him back in action again soon.

I have since been banned from Spurs Lodge and White Hart Lane and am not allowed within 100 metres of anyone connected with Tottenham Hotspur. I'm not bothered though. I will always love my Lilywhites from afar and will forever remember the day I discovered the secrets of the Lodge.

Monday December 12th 2005

FA Premiership
Tottenham Hotspur 3 Portsmouth 1
Attendance – 36,141
Spurs goalscorers: King, Mido (pen), Defoe

Tuesday December 13th 2005

AS THE BALL rolled over the line to crush Portsmouth's resistance, it became clear that Tottenham had found a leader who would not run from a battle. This is a story about the boy who would be King.

For years, there were rumblings among those in the know that there was something special coming through the Tottenham ranks. Opposition youth teams came away from matches against the young Spurs side talking about that amazing kid at the back. Dedicated fans knew there was a boy on his way who would one day become a superstar.

Ledley King joined Spurs as a 16-year-old trainee after starring for the East London amateur football giants Senrab. Playing alongside future stars including John Terry, Jlloyd Samuel, Paul Konchesky and on occasions current team-mate Jermain Defoe, it was often the quiet young defender who would prove the centre of conversation for crowds on the way back from the Wanstead Flats playing fields.

It would only be two years until the enormous clamour for his call-up to the first team was heard and the 18-year-old fledgling made his debut for the Lilywhites. He was used sparingly until the 2000/01 season when his form for the reserves and during his brief Premiership appearances meant that it was impossible to stop the strapping 6ft 2ins defender becoming a regular.

He played alongside a player he idolised in Sol Campbell and probably had no idea that his mentor was about to do a runner. When the surprise move across North London did take place in the summer of 2001, rather than run around like a headless chicken, Ledley used the departure to take his game to the next level.

Like Arthur waiting for his chance to pull out Excalibur, Ledley strode out onto the White Hart Lane pitch after the departure of Campbell and truly did become a King. He became everything the departed captain had been and then some. The crowd had a new hero to pin their hopes on. His impressive season culminated in his England debut against Italy in March 2002. The match was lost 2-1 but the class was there for the world to see.

Even Carrick Scored

Even though caretaker Spurs manager David Pleat tried his hardest to convert the boy into a defensive midfielder, he didn't grumble but turned it to his advantage. He became far more tactically aware, he learned to pass and move, he became assured on the ball and he even weighed in with some great goals, including one in the ill-fated cup match against Manchester City. All this after scoring the quickest goal in the Premiership.

Ironically enough, the match that would take Ledley King into the world-class bracket would see him partnered once again with the man who was there at the beginning. Sol Campbell, now hated by Spurs fans everywhere, would be the man that helped their hero through the best 90 minutes of his career so far. The result was once again a 2-1 loss but that match against France and the sight of the shackled Henry and Trezeguet was noticed around the world, not least by the big man standing in the French dugout.

He may have only spent a few weeks in Portugal but the Ledley King who returned to the Lane aged ten years in terms of experience and confidence. He gained an experienced central defensive partner and mentor in Noureddine Naybet and then saw his role reversed as he took the rising star, Michael Dawson, under his wing. Assured performances from both the young 'un and the slightly older 'un have made many pundits label them the best defensive partnership in the Premiership.

Ledley's rise has left Martin Jol, Sven Goran Eriksson and Spurs fans across North London rubbing their hands in glee. Don't say it too loudly in case the Russians hear but I think a new legend may have been unearthed at the Lane.

Sunday December 18th 2005

FA Premiership
Middlesbrough 3 Tottenham Hotspur 3
Attendance – 27,614
Spurs goalscorers: Keane, Jenas, Mido

FINALLY I CAN relax after holding my breath for far too long during periods of today's match and look forward to Christmas Day knowing that as well as loads of lovely presents to open, Tottenham Hotspur will be sitting proudly in fourth place.

As a festive gift, Martin and the boys have given us two games in the last six days boasting 10 goals, controversial incidents aplenty and – for the first time since Ossie – four strikers on the pitch at the same time. Now that's entertainment and means only two defeats in 17 games for the Lilywhites.

Against Portsmouth, we dominated but didn't turn possession into goals until the end of the game. However, for long periods today it was us who were under the cosh with corner after corner being fired into our box. The love handles of Viduka and the muscle of Yakubu meant that Middlesbrough's long balls were often held up on the edge of our area, allowing red shirts to overlap and cause Lee and Stalteri all sorts of problems.

The flipside to that coin though is that whereas Lua Lua's goal was a terrific long shot that would only possibly raise slightly harsh questions about Robbo's positioning, two of today's goals resulted from poor defending from set-pieces. Lee and Stalteri's lack of communication for the first goal left Yakubu alone for an easy finish while Dawson, although pushed, was unusually culpable in allowing Queudrue to outmuscle him in the air.

If you add the fact that Morrison seemed to ghost past

Dawson for the second goal then there'll certainly be some hard defensive drills going on in the next week. That's not to say the match was all about mistakes and downers at all. Once again that new Spurs grit and character reared its lovely head and kept up a fantastic record of coming from behind to snatch points.

Part of me is disappointed that we didn't pick up all three points and extend our victorious run today but I also remember that Manchester United, Liverpool and the Goons have all failed to win at the Riverside this season. The Devils and the French Fancies couldn't even take a point on their travels and taking into account our truly awful record at the ground, I'm not about to shed a white and navy tear.

That said, I very much doubt I was the only one on my feet, half celebrating, in that 90th minute when Defoe was clear through. Of all the people to wriggle through for a one-on-one, I wanted it to be Jermain, yet Mark Schwarzer's damn fat Aussie ankles stopped our collective glory. On a side note, it should be noted that it was Rasiak's headed flick that set up the opportunity.

The much-maligned Pole did everything asked of him when he came on and almost fashioned himself a fantastic individual effort in the dying minutes. He showed enough to suggest that the African Nations Cup won't be too disastrous for Spurs. He'll have his doubters until he gets a chance to prove himself properly. I'm not saying the man with as many Zs as Zsa Zsa was excellent in his short spell today but he certainly did not look a Championship player out of his depth as some have prematurely put it.

The man who will truly deserve all the praise tomorrow is Paul 'Octopus' Robinson. The shaven-headed saviour seems to get hands to shots he simply has no right to. If it wasn't for him then we would have lost heavily today. Cat-like doesn't do justice to the reflexes of England's Number One. I am beginning to suspect he is a robot sent back from the future to inspire Spurs fans across the world.

There were plenty of positives today. I thought Reid played well in the time allotted to him before he trudged off looking slightly miffed. Rather than a left-winger he appeared to be playing behind the front two on a number of occasions as well as getting across to link up with Lee and whip balls into the box. He worked tirelessly and he did a lot of running for a big man.

Davids was his usual force and was unlucky to pick up that early booking when he took the ball. His distribution was superb today and his presence is undoubtedly the difference now when we play away from the Lane. Nobody can afford to slacken off for fear of an Edgar rocket or a word to the bench that someone isn't pulling their weight.

Jermaine Jenas did well and his free kick was sublime. He does drift inside on too many occasions, leaving Stalteri with a lot to do, but his pace and energy going forward is like a shot in the arm to the team, especially on breakaways. Carrick beside him was neat and tidy and showed some good touches but failed to stamp his authority on the game as he has done in previous matches. Mido played with purpose and despite his usual tiring around the 60-minute mark, he still won the majority of his aerial battles.

As I've just remembered it, a word has to be said about Defoe's petulant moment after having that argument with the corner flag. What was the point in moaning like Kevin the teenager when all he had to do was pick up the damn corner flag? I understand it must be frustrating though to sit on the bench with the World Cup looming tantalisingly on the horizon, and Peter Crouch laughing at him from above, dancing in lederhosen.

However, while the Irishman keeps scoring scrappy goals, Defoe has to accept that the team must come first and not let it get on top of him. He may have thought he deserved to start today after scoring on Monday but his time will come again. In Defoe's defence, fans have to remember that Keane himself wasn't exactly averse to the odd act of petulance as the sub-striker last season when things weren't going his way.

If the little Englishman gets his chance on Boxing Day at any point, he may wish to remember that in the corresponding tie last season he scored one of his best individual efforts for Tottenham. Who's to say that lightning won't strike Steve Bruce's skull twice?

So I'm happy and when Martin sits around his table surrounded by Cock, Dick and one hell of a turkey on Sunday, I hope he realises he has ensured our team are not mid-table or on the edges of the European placings. They are fourth, above the Goons and in pole position for a continental sojourn next season.

Tottenham have smashed their own Premiership records along this fantastic start to the season and if our boys in white can kick off against Liverpool on January 14th with another clutch of wins behind them then our Champions League dreams may not be as far away as Mark Lawrenson and his red-tinted crew would like to think.

Monday December 26th 2005

FA Premiership
Tottenham Hotspur 2 Birmingham City 0
Attendance – 36,045
Spurs goalscorers: Keane (pen), Defoe

Tuesday December 27th 2005

I'M DISTRACTED BACK at work, my personal life is a mess, the earth is not quite spinning in the way it was before and I feel dizzy. All is not as it seems. Why? Well, it's pantomime season but Tottenham Hotspur are being far from comical and the reviews are all good.

In the last few seasons, I traditionally spent Christmas being teased mercilessly by numerous distant and ancient relatives, some who suspiciously look like nobody in the family, who were raised on the ultimate Spurs football of the late, great and impossible to emulate Bill Nicholson.

They queued up in an orderly fashion and proceeded to slap me with programmes from the 1960s before hobbling off, tripping the odd over-excited child with their deliberately placed slipper.

You find that for a lot of the old generation Tottenham fans, along with aching joints and a distinct loss of aim in the bathroom comes a mocking attitude to anything going on at White Hart Lane these days. While we current crop of Lilywhites live and breathe the new breed, we haven't tasted the success of our forebears. I suppose in a way that helps us identify with the new era coming in because together we want to create a new history for the club.

However, it's this new way that wreaked havoc with my Yuletide season. Last year, as with many before, I was taunted because the Tottenham philosophy was still seen as "we win some, we lose more". If there's a match we should have won then, by Jove, we'll cockerel it up big time.

But what's happened? Relatives dropped in presents in the Christmas build-up but there were no taunts, no laughing, not even a Jose Mourinho "I know I've lost but I won't admit it" smirk.

Even Carrick Scored

They threw the presents in and scampered off down the path, perhaps fearful that I'd mention the big Dutchman and use the J word.

I struggled to apply myself at work today. No more knuckling down to hard work because of a self-imposed internet strike brought on by another defensive calamity.

The grip on the mouse was only loosened when I realised that one small picture story on a fund-raising school fashion show was not going to cover my nine hours of Spurs rumour-scrounging and match report reading. It's funny that after a victory, those overused footballing clichés have never felt so fresh and invigorating.

But I'm scared. I've always said we'll win this game and then we'll beat so and so and we'll be that high in the league. How many others, like me, look at the league table frequently, work out what would happen if we won our next three or four games and completely overlook that other teams above us can win matches too?

Oh yeah, another 12 points and we're up there, no worries. It's that mindless passion for my team that has led to great amounts of finger pointing and riotous laughing in the streets. Well that and the fact that my wife once put a red top in the wash with my Spurs home shirt.

This is the bit where I'm going to have to whisper so they can't hear me and lock me up again. I think I'm controlling events at White Hart Lane. I wanted a load of old crap cleared out from the club and it was. I once asked for David Pleat to be dumped in a bin outside Highbury and he was. I asked for a tough boss to grab the club by the throat and shake any overpaid laziness out of it and that seems to be happening, but most of all I asked for some consistency and at least one special winger and we may finally be getting that too.

Shhh... Someone's coming... (Louder now) What I meant to say of course was that now we seem to have a set-up in place at the club which is either listening to the fans or has enough sense to spot weaknesses and address them. We're beating teams now we're supposed to and even the most insidious of newspapers are impressed with Jol's turnaround of our fortunes.

Yes I am scared because there's a long way to go but it's really that nervous kind of excitement that comes before you leap into something new and thrilling. If life as a Spurs fan is a rollercoaster ride then us younger ones have been travelling slowly along a rubbish flat bit with the odd bump that makes you chip your teeth on the safety bar.

You know what though, we're tilting upwards now. Looking around I can see all the shocked faces of other young Lilywhites. Near the front I can see Ledley, Robbo and little Aaron with an icecream and who's that in the front carriage, with their arms on each other's shoulders singing "Glory, Glory"? It looks like a giant Dutchman and a little bald chairman crooning to one another.

I paid for this seat 26 years ago and even when it's been boring and I've stared out through tearful eyes at other attractions, I've never wanted to get off. Many have said that before I got on, there was a time when the ride hit its summit. If that's the case then like a certain Mr Wonka's elevator, I'm hoping this ride is on its way to smash through that barrier and into orbit.

Wednesday December 28th 2005

FA Premiership
West Bromwich Albion 2 Tottenham Hotspur 0
Attendance – 27,510

Thursday December 29th 2005

AS I DON'T want my still lingering festive cheer to be ruined by dissecting a muted performance against West Brom, here are some major Hollywood movies the Tottenham way. I've tried to stay as faithful to the original scripts as possible and transplanted them.

LEON

ASSASSIN DAMIEN COMOLLI is sitting on a roof-top with young Jermain Defoe, who he reluctantly rescued from a shooting in North London. He is pushing him with his index finger.

DC: Painful, eh? It's zis fear that makes you miss. It's because you fear death that you play with so much tenacity. It's because of it that you bear what's unbearable. You can live in a hovel in White Hart Lane, on lots of trash; everything is better than death and the fear you have of it.

JD: But…

DC: But me… Damien… I don't fear it any more… It takes a long time to lose it, this fear, but once you lose it… You are free… And just then you can start playing properly… Because you can work on other people's fear, play with it… Because kill or get killed have become just words and it is time to put the ball in the goal. Oui? Do you understand?

JD: Yes, sir.

DC: Good boy, now drink your milk.

THE SIXTH SENSE

ANDY REID IS sitting in a bed in Great Ormond Street Hospital. Noureddine Naybet has come in to visit him with grapes.

AR: I want to tell you my secret now.

NN: OK.

AR: I see people... I see dead people... Some of them scare me.

NN: In your dreams? When you're awake? (Andy nods) Dead people, like in graves and coffins?

AR: No, walking around, like regular people... They can't see each other. Some of them don't know they're finished.

NN: How often do you see them?

AR: All the time. They're everywhere. You won't tell anyone my secret, right? (Naybet shakes his head). Will you stay here till I fall asleep?

(The Moroccan nods and tucks him in. Through Andy's hospital room window we see the adjacent wing of the hospital building. Three windows are visible. The ghostly figures of Goran Bunjevcevic, Johnnie Jackson and Dean Marney are staring at the little Irishman. He screws his eyes shut and tries to sleep.)

JAWS

SOL CAMPBELL IS talking to his Arsenal team-mates during the match against Spurs on April 22nd 2006. Jermain Defoe is flying towards the former Lilywhite, Kolo Toure and Lauren with the ball.

SC: See what I do, chief, is I trick him to the surface, then I jab at him! I'm not gonna haul him up like a load of catfish. Kolo! Full throttle!

KT: I don't have to take this abuse much longer!

L: (Looking at Campbell) Hey, your head's bleedin'! First-aid there. Let Kolo take a turn.

SC: Stop playin' with yerself, Kolo. Slow ahead, if you please.

L: You heard him, slow ahead!... Slow ahead! I can go slow ahead! C'mon down and chum some of this shit!

(Jermain Defoe jinks right past all of them and smashes the ball past Jens Lehmann.

L: You're gonna need a bigger defence!

THE TERMINATOR

ARSÈNE WENGER IS talking to Pat Rice in a bar in London when suddenly Martin Jol bursts in and starts throwing people out of the way as he treads a path towards the two Gooners.

AW: Come with me if you want to live.

PR: Oh my god!

(They run across the room as Martin smashes through men and furniture. Wenger and Rice run down a corridor and into the kitchen. They hit a closed door which crashes open. As Rice runs off, Wenger turns and bolts the door.

An instant later the door is blown off its hinges. Martin begins to sprint down the corridor into the alley where the two gooners have run. Rice stumbles over trash cans while Wenger pulls him mercilessly along. They steal a car and drive off. Martin is running effortlessly like a panther behind them. However, they pull away.)

AW: Are you injured? Are you shot?

PR: This is a mistake. I haven't done anything. How could that man do that?

AW: He's not a man. Cyberdyne Systems Model 101. Martin Jol is an infiltration unit. Part man, part machine. Underneath, he's got a combat chassis, hyperalloy, fully armoured. Very tough. Built to construct the ultimate football team. But outside, there's living human tissue. Flesh, skin, hair, well, some hair, and blood.

(He swerves the car round a corner.)

PR: I don't understand.

AW: Listen. Understand. Martin Jol is out there. He can't be reasoned with, can't be bargained with... he doesn't feel pity or remorse or fear for other clubs...and absolutely will not stop... Ever... Until every one of us Gooners is dead.

(They both slump in resignation.)

Saturday December 31st 2005

FA Premiership
Tottenham Hotspur 2 Newcastle United 0
Attendance – 36,246
Spurs goalscorers: Tainio, Mido

Chapter Seven

January
Last Minute Lameness

Wednesday January 4th 2006

FA Premiership
Manchester City 0 Tottenham Hotspur 2
Attendance – 40,808
Spurs goalscorers: Mido, Keane

Thursday January 5th 2006

THROUGH THE DRIVING snow and bitter cold, I trudged across the Scottish Highlands in a desperate search for a pub, farmhouse or even a hermit's hut that could pick up Sky Sports. I was trying not to think about the fact that I had borrowed my wife's car and left it for dead halfway up a steep snow-covered hill.

It was 8.05pm and my Tottenham could be flying or dying against Manchester City, but here I was walking across a dark, dank field with an oddly-coloured mixture of snow and cow crap gathering on my trouser legs. A week in the company of my parents, north of the border, was swiftly going downhill after a happy Hogmanay.

"Don't worry, honey, I'm sure somewhere will have the game on," I'd shouted jovially as I strained to close the door behind me in the Arctic blast. An hour later and a car lighter, I was ruing my optimism while swiping away small icicles that had formed on my eyelashes.

Ode to Jol

The two pubs I'd found while driving had proved to be deadends. The red-cheeked rotund landlady in one had simply laughed at me and told me they weren't "that kind of establishment". In the other, a tiny pub that looked on the verge of collapse, I walked into a scene of desolation. A small, squinting, balding man stood grinning strangely behind the bar, barely tall enough to pull a pint, while an old, bearded man sat on a stool arguing with his sheepdog.

There was no television in sight and the fact that the bar area smelt as if a previous unfortunate drifter had been stabbed, chopped up, then eaten and farted out by the sheepdog gave me cause to smile politely while edging quickly back out of the old oak door.

So here I was, clambering over yet another snow-soaked stile in my pursuit of happiness. Then it happened... An orange glow appeared on the horizon and big Martin was there frantically screaming instructions my way and pointing in the direction of a nearby hill. My wife would later try to tell me that the glow was from a streetlight and that the vision came because I was a loon.

She may be right on both counts but that doesn't legislate for the welcome appearance of the Hope and Glory Inn, standing alone in the middle of nowhere, over that very hill. I sloshed across the 500m separating me from my destiny and crashed through the doors – much to the consternation of the handful of drinkers sprinkled inside the watering hole.

The group of farmers and eccentric-looking locals looked me up and down and then turned back to a small television, balanced delicately on two large books in the corner of the bar. My head whipped around as the name "Mido" boomed from the little set. The people of this little warm and toasty pub, in the middle of a land that might as well have been Middle Earth or Narnia to me, were watching the mighty Lilywhites and we'd only gone and bloody scored.

I ordered myself a pint of the local brew and found myself a good seat next to the radiator – not before the smiling landlord told me that he'd had Sky installed only the previous week, after years of resisting it, because the pub couldn't get terrestrial reception in the worsening winter weather.

So to the game. Gone were the Spurs of The Hawthorns and back were the new, resilient Jolly Babies. Barring a last minute cross-cum-shot from Bradley Wright-Phillips, Paul Robinson didn't have a save to make. That was testament as much to the future England international Michael Dawson as to Anthony Gardner.

I am not one of Big Tony's most ardent fans and still believe that with the ball at his feet he looks shakier than Graeme Souness' grip on his St James' Park desk.

However, even the Highland locals agreed that Lurch's long-lost brother had a cracking game, putting in Dawsonesque last-ditch tackles all over the shop. Andy Cole was made to look his age while Darius Vassell was made to look like the no-necked penalty-misser he was at Villa.

The right-sided partnership of Paul Stalteri and Aaron Lennon proved once again that it can bear fruit. Stalteri's tough tackling and support play were the perfect springboard for the lightning-soled Oompa Loompa's forays into the opposition half. Jermaine Jenas enjoyed a more central role as a result of that and he and Carrick dominated the engine room for most of the match, with Joey Barton feeding off scraps.

Mido once again proved he has no match in the air and his partnership with Keane continues to grow, much to little Jermain's frustration on the bench. How many assists have the two given each other in recent games?

I've made no secret of the fact that the diminutive striker is the main man in my eyes, but even I'd be loath to fix what ain't broke right now.

As Keane's sweet finish sealed a fine festive fixture list for Spurs, I was left staring into my pint, dreaming what might just be.

The gap is growing behind us rather than in front of us. For once a breakaway group of top teams includes the side from N17 not N5. Can we do it? Can we reach the Euro-soaked promised land? Will we entertain the likes of Barcelona at White Hart Lane next year? Even a visit from Tromso on a floodlit Uefa Cup night would get my juices flowing.

If a wafer-thin squad like Liverpool's can win the Champions League then who's to say our Lilywhites aren't ready for a European adventure in some shape or form? However, while we can afford to gain a little confidence from our new-look side, we still know that with Tottenham anything can happen and invariably does.

We've broken a slew of our own Premiership records and now is the time for concentration and consolidation to ensure we are still there at the end of the season, rather than missing out by a few measly points to some little Northern side with no grand history lining its stadium's corridors.

I finished the dregs of my pint and left the handful of locals with a brief lecture on the importance of having a big squad with fresh players fighting to remain in a hotly-contested first eleven. Leaving them looking slightly puzzled at my waffling, I buttoned up my coat, flicked up the collar and stepped out on a far happier return hike to my car.

The swirling snow had lessened to a light fall and I used up the final bars of power on my phone to call the

RAC and tell them to meet me at my wife's deceased car. I gave them the name of the pub as a guide. Two hours later, while listening to Radio 5 in the stationary vehicle, I was startled by a knock on the window.

It was the RAC man, who proceeded to explain that he'd been driving around the white-blanketed countryside for the last hour and had searched everywhere for the Hope and Glory Inn. It wasn't anywhere on his satellite navigation system and none of the local pubs he had stopped at had heard of it. He had eventually found my stricken vehicle by taking a lucky turn.

I was thinking about the pub on the bumpy journey back to my parents' home when a smile began to form on my cold and battered lips. I looked out the dark window at the white, undulating snow and struck up the Champions League music in my head. No Hope and Glory? You've got to be kidding, mate, I'm a Lilywhite.

Sunday January 8th 2006

FA Cup 3rd Round
Leicester 3 Tottenham Hotspur 2
Attendance – 19,844
Spurs goalscorers: Jenas, Stalteri

Thursday January 12th 2006

IT'S TAKEN ME four days of counselling and tender love and care to finally emerge from my black, black mood after the lameness of our last-minute loss to Leicester; yes, I did say Leicester. My psychiatrist has told me not to talk any further about the fact that we have crashed out of yet another cup competition to a last-minute goal against lower-league opposition.

So you know what, I'm going to take that advice.

Screw the present and my wish to decapitate everyone within a mile of my hands. Screw Mark De Vries and the best game of his career. Screw the world. Redrum, redrum, redrum... I must stop!

I say lock the lot of them in a room with tapes of all of the double-winning side's matches and the words of Bill Nicholson and only let them out if they are ready to give the fans something back for all their years of optimistic unwarranted support.

Normal optimistic service will be resumed in the next few days when I calm down and rediscover my inspiration. As you can tell, I am in a very dark place right now and I apologise for the ugliness of my words.

Instead of dissecting the lameness, I'm going to take a dewy-eyed look back to the recent past and two of the men who were there at the beginning of the White Hart Lane revolution.

I want to pay tribute to the underrated and underused pair of midfielders I once dubbed The Odd Couple. Pedro Mendes and Sean Davis are Spurs no more after they signed for Portsmouth today.

One was a skinhead from London, the other was a long-haired Lothario from Portugal. Before July 10th 2004, neither Sean Davis nor Pedro Miguel da Silva Mendes had probably ever set eyes on each other. One could be found plying his trade at the Estádio do Dragão winning league titles, cups and the Champions League. You know, the usual stuff. The other could be seen treading the blades of grass at the home of Championship side Queen's Park Rangers. Enough said.

In those very different days, neither would believe it if you told them they were going to become the engine room of a new-look Tottenham Hotspur side. However, it wasn't long until the pair seemed as if they'd been playing together since they were little kids with jumpers for goalposts.

Last Minute Lameness

I remember my first experience of White Hart Lane, after the Santini/Jol/Arnesen arrival last season, was the match against Birmingham. The first thing I noticed when the team came out to warm up before the match was two players away from the crowd. After the initial jogs, Sean and Pedro excused themselves and came over close to the East Stand and began a bit of a ritual.

They passed to each other, they ran past each other, they laid the ball off to each other. Like two mates in a park, they were enjoying themselves and were showing their instant understanding.

Both players were instinctively touching the ball to where they knew the other would be. This continued for fifteen minutes and was to be the pattern for the game. When Spurs were pressing forward, the two were linking brilliantly and setting up attacks.

When we were on the back foot, they were flying in with challenges. Not the rubbish attacker running back challenges we'd been used to at the Lane, but real bone-shuddering tackles that swept the ball away and stamped their authority over their counterparts.

When it came to passing, both had their specialities. Davis liked to spray the ball across the park, while Mendes preferred lots of flicks and intelligent link-up play. The styles completely complemented each other.

When the 90 minutes were done and the three points were in the bag, Mendes saluted the fans on his way into the tunnel and Davis went one step further by coming over to each end of the stadium and acknowledging the support. It was wholeheartedly returned.

This new engine room continued until Santini ran for the French hills and a young contender called Michael Carrick entered the fray. Injuries would take their toll on Davis and, barring the night at Old Trafford when Pedro did what Pele couldn't, Mendes soon became a back-up man.

However, their introduction cannot be overlooked in the Tottenham revolution. Before them, when was the last time we had a strong partnership in the middle of the pitch? I'm struggling to think of one and I'm going back years. We always seemed to have two individuals, or an injury-hit pairing, or a makeshift midfielder stolen from the defence, attack or wing to make up numbers. If anything they were the precursor to the mighty superstar Pitbull.

You may not see the Lambeth anchorman or the Guimaraes battler sharing a cultured bottle of wine together in a Portuguese restaurant or 'avin it large in an East End nightclub, but on the pitch I wish the best to them both and hope The Odd Couple continue to cement their partnership in the Premiership.

Saturday January 14th 2006

FA Premiership
Liverpool 1 Tottenham Hotspur 0
Attendance – 44,983

Wednesday January 18th 2006

WHILE NOBODY CAN deny the progress made at N17 this season, it would be difficult to counter the claim that although solid we don't create enough chances.

Some sides play through a creative link man, an attacking midfielder with the energy to sweep forward into the box, setting up the strikers or running in unmarked to power the ball home.

When Martin Jol took over the helm at Spurs, he made

it clear that he favoured the other source of creation – wingers. To hopefully start a debate, I'm suggesting that the big Dutchman's dream has been tied up and shot to pieces by the club's signing policy.

Jol's plan was that with two defensive midfielders sweeping up all before them in the middle of the park, two nimble out-and-out wingers are left free to terrorise the full-backs before whipping cross after cross into the box. With Carrick and Davids, Jol already has two of the best in the defensive business at his disposal.

However, the influx of other quality central midfielders such as Teemu Tainio and Jermaine Jenas has forced the big man's hand. Rumours of a Levy-enforced signing of the Newcastle midfielder on the recommendation of Sven have always circled. How can Jol leave out a £7m signing or the aggressive, energetic Finn? The result has seen The Pitbull muzzled out on the left side either of a flat four or the world-renowned diamond formation – also known as the 'how do I fit in all these quality central midfielders?' formation.

The diamond formation essentially sucks acres of width away from a team, leaving the only crosses into the box coming from energetic full-backs, who are required to sprint up and down the channels every match. There's little doubt that Jenas is growing with each game or that Tainio is a top player who plays with his heart on his sleeve, but nobody should be wedged into a team.

I think Spurs are at the stage now where we don't have to crowbar all our stars into the first eleven – as Jermain Defoe has discovered. Barring injury or an enforced formation change, central midfielders, however good or expensive they are, should fight it out for those two slots in the middle. Why wasn't a left-winger bought in the summer?

Throughout the history of football, a true winger has

been the key to unlocking any team's defence, however resolute. Even the best defender in the world can be turned inside out by genuine skill and unpredictability. How many times this season have you heard commentators salivating over the pace and skill of Aaron Lennon?

His final ball does need work, but he's scared every single left-back he's come across and Mido must love playing with him, knowing that if the kid's on the ball it's worth sprinting into the box for a possible cut back or cross. It's true that with his age and size, the supersonic Oompa Loompa can fade from games, but with a winger of equal pace and threat on the left, the responsibility wouldn't be heaped on the youngster's shoulders and chances would abound.

Jol's formations appear to attempt to stifle the opposition first, dominate the midfield, stroke it about and hope something happens up front. Spurs have grown enough in stature to stop thinking so much about the other team and let them worry about the Lilywhites rampaging towards them.

Against Liverpool, despite Jol's admission that he thought it was to be Spurs' day, we created just three decent chances. I'm not knocking the midfielders who all did their job in controlling the centre of the park, but if we want to make the next level we have to create against the top teams.

Jamie Carragher said straight after the game that Tottenham were one of the hardest teams Liverpool have faced this season in any competition. I think he meant more in getting past us and winning the ball from us in midfield, not that he and his defensive line had to face an onslaught of Spurs chances.

So who's missing on that left side? Andy Reid hasn't been given the greatest of chances to impress but even Jol has admitted he's more of a left-footed central

After the infamous Highbury 'injury' and goal, Martin Jol ironically tells Arsene Wenger he "did not see it".

Damien Comolli tells Sven about a kid called Aaron.

Bolton keeper Jussi Jaaskelainen can only look on as Aaron Lennon jinks through and scores at the Lane.

Martin Jol signs off at White Hart Lane with a 1-0 win against Bolton.

The Lilywhites are heading back into Europe.

Martin Jol realises his sick Spurs have lost Champions League football at Upton Park.

A glimpse of the future? Aaron Lennon comes on for David Beckham against Portugal.

New signings Benoit Assou-Ekotto, Dimitar Berbatov and Didier Zokora show the future and the new kits.

midfielder. Another suggestion is playing both Lennon and Routledge with one on the left or them continually switching. That could work but doesn't create a natural balance.

The recently mooted idea is to bring Wayne Bridge in and push Lee Young-Pyo up into midfield. Ordinarily that would work, but our incredibly right-footed left-back would nine times out of ten head infield rather than beat his man and whip the ball in. The main option is to buy someone special for that left spot, a Vicente, Ribery or Denilson type, although that type of player rarely becomes available in January.

The most unfortunate thing of all is that the closest we have to a skilful left-winger, who has already scared many Premiership right-backs, is sitting on a bench in Germany staring befuddled at the terrifying skills of Thimothee Atouba. Reto Ziegler was our Lennon-type find last year, yet he was sent away, cast into the mire. If a major falling out didn't happen between him and Jol in the summer, then are we to expect the same of Lennon next year? Will he be put on a train to Outer Mongolia for experience?

Ziegler on one side with Lennon or Routledge on the other. Sounds pretty exciting to me, especially with the bite and savvy of Davids/Tainio and Carrick/Jenas in the middle. If the swish Swiss star can be recalled halfway through his unhappy season-long spell then it would surely be as good as a new signing this window.

Whoever the leftie, I'm calling on you, Martin, to look to the sides and let wingers blast apart our opposition. Don't let the money men pull down your vision before it's been built – ignore them and bring balance to the force.

Saturday January 21st 2006

FA Premiership
Tottenham Hotspur 0 Aston Villa 0
Attendance – 36,243

Monday January 23rd 2006

DAMN SORENSON AND his goal-sized gloves. I've been moaning all weekend about our inability to score on Saturday. I moaned at fellow fans in the stadium and my family heard the rest on Sunday so I'm not going to bore the world by whinging about it any more. Instead I'm going to talk about another side to supporting Tottenham Hotspur. The side that has nothing to do with what happens on the pitch.

The dictionary describes speculation as reasoning based on inconclusive evidence, conjecture or supposition. Yes it may be but why should that get in the way of a juicy bit of gossip?

At the beginning of this month I woke up, the sun was shining and some small irritating birds were singing in my ear. So I reached over and turned off the Sugababes blaring on the radio and stared out of the window for a moment. My head was still buzzing from the previous night's antics but something was nagging away at me, something deep inside that I was supposed to remember.

New Year's Day... January 1st... Oh my god, the start of the transfer window. The covers were thrown off and a frantic dive was made straight over to the computer to find out what global superstars Tottenham had been linked with on this very special day.

There's something contagious about transfer speculation. Even the cheapest, nastiest rumour can spread between men faster than syphilis in an Amsterdam brothel. A man called Clive, living in a wardrobe in the Shetland Islands, can post a story on the net claiming that his brother's nephew's dog saw Damien Comolli and Ronaldo in a café in Paris and within hours the web goes into meltdown.

Tottenham Hotspur are particularly prone to these Chinese whispers. Bryan Adams may have had his Summer of '69 but he never experienced the heady summers of Rivaldo, Morientes and Davids. Like Johnnie Jackson and reserve-team football, gossip seems made for Spurs and you know what? I love it.

At least 99% of me knows that if the Daily Rag says that Martin Jol is meeting Fernando Torres in Madrid over a shock move, it's complete drivel.

That doesn't mean that the other one per cent can't revel in the excitement of the possibilities. I know a source within the club or a close friend of the player is really Bob, the bloke who sits across the desk from the journalist who wrote the piece, but isn't it all so exciting?

The transfer window means all transfer activity is crowbarred into one month of frenzied anticipation. A second mini-summer if you will. I don't care if you're eight, 18 or 80, the mere mention of a world-class player coming to your club should be enough for your heart to skip a beat. It's half of what being a fan is all about.

The cynical ones will say we're only setting ourselves up for a fall but they don't understand. It's about the dream. It's about having 11 players on that pitch that you just know every other fan in the country is salivating messily over. Experience has taught us enough to not expect Torres to join but that should never ever stop us daydreaming about the what ifs.

Ode to Jol

Half of being a supporter is urging your players on to success on the pitch week in week out, but the other half is enjoying the sometimes outrageous speculation that pokes up its flirtatious head in between matches. Newspapers ruthlessly exploit those of us who thrive on the rumours but are we ever going to say "no more"? Show me one fan whose heart doesn't beat faster reading stories linking us with Christian Vieri, Raphael Van Der Vaart, Wesley Sneijder and Shaun Wright-Phillips and I shall pronounce him dead.

I'm aware that quartet would cost a combined fee of around £45m and would be almost half a title-challenging side but don't bother me with the facts. We may live and love football but that's because it's so bloody enjoyable not because we take every moment truly seriously. If that was the case, a mob of torch-carrying fans would have already marched to Rob Styles' home and hung him before carrying out a mass suicide on his lawn.

If your support for Tottenham could be symbolised as a Belgian Bun, then the transfer speculation is the shiny cherry on top. The Charlton and Fulham fans of this world can laugh at us all they like when we talk up another possibility because to be brutally honest they'll never be big enough to be linked with these kinds of players themselves. Sad but true.

We all know the annual David Beckham rumour that goes round is about as likely to occur as Posh having another number one hit. But does that stop even the most cynical of Spurs fans from debating whether he'd fit into Martin Jol's plans and whether he'd be good for the image of the club? Of course it doesn't and deep down everyone loves the buzz that comes with it.

So if you're like me and regularly flick on Sky Sports News, Teletext, the internet, or even grab newspapers in shops with a relish that causes other customers to edge back a little and small children to hide behind their mothers' legs, then, fear not, you are not alone.

We don't play for Spurs, we don't manage them, and the heavy-handed local police won't even let us shout instructions up at Martin Jol's office window. So by the only power vested in me, I am bloody well going to speculate, wonder and revel in the delicious rumours which come as a side dish with the feast that is Tottenham Hotspur.

Sunday January 29th 2006

SEIZING AN OPPORTUNITY, whenever it comes, can often define a footballer's career. The great and the good revel in the moment, while those who stutter and stumble are rapidly consigned to the Premiership scrapheap.

The walls of White Hart Lane are adorned with the images of Lilywhites who saw their chance looming before them and grabbed it with both hands. Outside the stadium, in the dark, dank alleyways of Tottenham High Street lie the crumpled posters of those who came, saw and slipped away into obscurity. They have learned the hard way that football is not a patient game.

Yesterday, beer in hand, I was talking over the chances of seeing Lee Barnard in the Spurs first team. A friend reminded me that the prolific young reserve striker had featured on the bench on at least one occasion a couple of years ago. I began to wonder whether Barnard had never been given a real chance or had he blown the lesser opportunities he'd had to shine?

Despite his superb tally in reserve football, his league record does not read well at all. Loans at Exeter, Stevenage Borough, Leyton Orient and Northampton have seen him play 23 times with a solitary goal for Boro. While the fans' clamour to have the youngster in the team has always been there, the harsh question would be: is he likely to score in the Premiership if he has struggled to do so in League Two and the Conference?

In his favour, it has been announced today that he's signed a new two-year deal this weekend – despite Jol's feeling at the fans' Q and A that he would leave in the summer. This may suggest that with his continued reserve goals, the club still believes there is a possibility he could get another chance to make the grade in the future. Having seen him in action for the reserves, I hope the youngster grabs it if it comes along.

Conversely, while Barnard stuttered in the league, his reserve team-mate, 19-year-old left-footed, yes left-footed, midfielder Jamie O'Hara has sparkled in his loan spell for Chesterfield in League One. I saw that in only his third game yesterday, he notched up his first ever professional goal, a top corner screamer from the edge of the area to snatch a win against Bournemouth. His performances have been creating a buzz in the Peak District and while it's not guaranteed that he'll return to take Tottenham by storm, he'll certainly be ticking all the boxes for the watching Spurs scout.

The example for both is the fast-tracked Phil Ifil, who used others' injuries to his benefit at the start of last season and has continued to develop in the Championship with Millwall at pace with that extra slice of experience. With Stephen Kelly showing an apparent unwillingness to wait for his moment, the young Englishman could have a special part to play in the coming years.

The trio of reserves got me thinking about others who have taken or spurned chances when they came – for one reason or another. In the summer, we signed

Wayne Routledge to replace Simon Davies and brought in Aaron Lennon as a youngster to develop among the reserves. Five months on and Routledge is turning out for the reserves, while Lennon grabbed his chance and has thus far sprinted so fast that no one stands a chance of taking it off him.

Injury robbed Routledge of his early months at Spurs, but when he gets another chance will he be ready or will he fade and grumble? Conflicting recent quotes from him leave me divided as to which camp he will fall in. As the old cliché says, I hope the youngster keeps his head down, trains hard and prepares for his time. He'd better, as I heavily tipped him in the summer to become our right-sided Ginola.

Mido and Grzegorz Rasiak are another study of different paths. The Egyptian strolled confidently onto the scene with a scintillating brace that caught the fans' and media's attention. The entrance masked the fact that he struggled for the rest of his first season. The Pole, however, had a goal ruled out and hit the bar with another effort on his debut. Against Villa, he had a snapshot that could have kick-started his Tottenham career and won the game, but it was blocked as he tried to dig the shot out.

The line that separates success and failure is desperately thin. Sometimes bad luck can be the difference between a chance being taken or spurned. Had Rasiak notched up two goals on his debut, his confidence and the fans' treatment of him would have been a world apart from where they are now. Nobody would be talking about offloading him after a couple of months. Judging by his 19 goals last season, he has tremendous ability on the deck and in the air but will he get the chance to show that?

It's no coincidence that the majority of the current

Spurs stars took their opportunity when it came. Without any reserve games under his belt, Michael Dawson came in for the injured Naybet at Anfield last season, took all the plaudits and hasn't looked back since. As for the man alongside him, although he had already begun to feature, Ledley King came to the fore when he filled the slot left when Campbell departed for The Library.

Even established performers such as Robbo, Defoe and Lee all grabbed their early opportunities for Spurs and their countries. Carrick waited patiently for his chance before shining when it eventually came under Jol.

History contains pages full of those who have benefited or suffered at the expense of others. Probably the most famous chance-grabber of all had his moment at the expense of one of our legends. Were it not for injury and a certain World Cup hat-trick hero in 1966, Sir Jimmy Greaves could have become the nation's darling, not just ours.

For a young player there is nothing more important than breaking through with style and confidence. While an established pro may get more time to sparkle, i.e. Robbie Keane and Thierry Henry, the game is a harsh place for those coming through. So many upcoming prospects have faded from the scene in recent years with less than a whimper. Names such as Rory Allen, Neale Fenn, Ben Bowditch, Alton Thelwell, Mark Gower, Jamie Slabber and Owen Price have all been cast aside from the top tier despite the players' early promise. Admittedly, a few of those didn't get the chance to make the step up to the first team, but it's always been drummed into me that you earn your opportunities in life and when you get them, you take them.

It remains to be seen whether the current crop of El-Hamdaoui, Huddlestone, O'Hara, McKenna and Mills will make that difficult step up and whether experienced performers like Routledge, Kelly, Davenport, Reid and Rasiak will take a second chance if it comes their way. With the revival going on at White Hart Lane and the prospect of European football and with it the need for a large squad, now is the time to step up to the plate and deliver for club and career.

Tuesday January 31st 2006

FA Premiership
Fulham 1 Tottenham Hotspur 0
Attendance – 21,081

I REFUSE TO even discuss the fact that we let in another bloody last-minute goal again tonight. You could just see it coming in another one of those muted, "I'm not sure what to do" performances. So I am going to escape to the world of the movies once again with a slight Tottenham Hotspur twist. I'm not going to add the titles this time as it's more fun to work them out.

Martin Jol walks into Damien Comolli's kitchen one morning wearing a long black coat and sporting some very snazzy sunglasses.

DC: I'd ask you to sit down, but you're not going to anyway. And don't worry about the trophy.

MJ: What trophy? (He turns around and his elbow knocks a Premiership trophy from the table. It falls to the floor.) Ah crap, I'm sorry.

DC: I said don't worry about it. I'll get one of my kids to fix it.

MJ: How did you know?

Damien sets a cookie tray on a wooden hot-pad.

DC: What's really going to bake your noodle later

on is, would you still have broken it if I hadn't said anything... So? What do you think? You think you're the one?

MJ: I don't know.

Damien gestures to a wooden plaque with words in Latin.

DC: You know what that means? It's Latin. Means, 'To dare is to do'. (He puts his cigarette down) Well, let's have a look at you.

He widens the big man's eyes, checks his ears, then feels the glands in his neck.

DC: Open your mouth. Say, "ahhh". (He nods then looks at his palms.) Hmmm. You sure got the gift, but it's tricky. I'd say the bad news is, you're not the one. Still got a lot to learn. Maybe next life.

MJ: What's the good news?

DC: You're not David Pleat.

MJ: Is that it, then?

DC: No. Here. (He picks up the tray of cooling cookies.) You better take one, got a big season ahead of you.

Martin looks at Damien, and then takes the whole plate of cookies.

MJ: You're wrong. I am the one.

He looks up and flies through the ceiling. Damien looks up through the smashed hole.

DC: He just had to believe.

Martin Jol and Sir Alex Ferguson meet in a café halfway between Manchester and Holland late during the night where the big man has just explained that he can't be Fergie's assistant as he wants to manage Tottenham one day.

AF: I do what I do best. I win league titles. You want

to do what you do best trying to stop guys like me.

MJ: You never wanted a normal-type life?

AF: What the hell is that? Barbecues and ball games?

MJ: That's part of it.

AF: That's nice. That your life?

MJ: No. My wife spends half her time on the couch. My stepdaughter's got problems because her real father's a world-class arsehole. And every moment I got, I'm chasing guys like you.

AF: A man told me once, you want to be a top manager, don't keep anything in your life you're not willing to walk out on in 30 seconds flat if you feel the heat around the corner. So if you're chasing me and you gotta move when I move, how do you expect to keep a family?

MJ: What are you, a monk?

AF: No. I got a woman.

MJ: What do you tell her?

AF: She thinks I sell swimming pools.

MJ: And if my team give yours a thumping one day, you gonna walk out on her? Leave her flat like that? Not even say goodbye?

AF: That's the discipline.

MJ: What you're left with is pretty empty.

AF: Yeah? Then maybe you and me, we should both go do something else, pal.

MJ: I don't know how to do anything else.

AF: Neither do I.

MJ: And I don't much want to.

AF: Neither do I.

MJ: We're sitting here like a couple of regular fellas. You do what you do. I do what I gotta do. What happens if I am there and I got to put your team away? I won't like it. But, if it's between them and my side then you are gonna go down.

AF: There's a flip side to that coin. What if you got them boxed in and I gotta put you down? Because no matter what, you will not get in my way. But now that we been face to face, I would not feel good about that. But I won't hesitate. Not for one second.

MJ: Maybe it'll happen that way. Or…

AF: Maybe it won't.

They look at each other for a moment with a wry smile as if they both know they'll meet again one day.

Big Edgar and Little Aaron walk into a solarium in London.

ED: Son, have a look under that one. (Aaron looks under one of the sunbeds and Jose Mourinho is lying there.)

AL: Sleeping like a baby.

Edgar approaches and raises the sunbed. Jose's eyes widen as the Dutchman slams down the sunbed on top of him.

ED: Got some bad news for you, Jose.

JM: What the fu-!

Edgar slams it down again.

ED: Mind your language in front of my boy.

JM: Jesus Christ!

Edgar repeats the earlier treatment twice more.

ED: That includes blasphemy as well. Now tell me, Jose…

JM: Tell you what?

ED: Tell me Jose, how you can concentrate on improving a lovely tan, and it is a lovely tan by the way, when you have more pressing priorities at hand?

JM: Tell Martin…

Bang, as the sunbed comes down again.

ED: Did I say speak? And it's Mr Jol to you. Now don't disappoint me and choose your words carefully. You may speak.

JM: I'll have the three points for Mr Jol in a couple of weeks. I have been busy. No chance of you lifting this sunbed up is there?

ED: Yeah, all right. (He lifts it, then smashes it down again.) Now, you want me to lift it up again? (Jose shakes his head.) You be at the Bridge at 12.45pm on March 11th and don't be late.

He punches the little manager unconscious, turns up the time dial and the pair walk out.

Martin Jol is sitting at his desk with Chris Hughton and Clive Allen sitting in other chairs in the room. Joe Kinnear is shown into the room and tells Martin that he needs a job.

MJ: Why didn't you come to me first when we spoke about Andy?

JK: What do you want of me now? Tell me anything. But do what I beg you to do.

MJ: What is that? (Joe gets up to whisper his request into Martin's ear.) That I cannot do.

JK: I'll give you anything you ask.

MJ: We've known each other many years, but this is the first time you came to me for counsel, for help. I can't remember the last time that you invited me to your house for a cup of coffee, even though my wife is godmother to your only child. But you never wanted my friendship and you were afraid to be in my debt.

JK: I didn't want to get into trouble.

MJ: I understand. You found paradise in Nottingham, had a good job, made a good living and you didn't need a friend of me. But now you come to me and you say "Don Jol give me justice". But you don't ask with respect. You don't offer friendship. You don't even think to call me Godfather. Instead, you come into my office on the day of my daughter's wedding and you ask for work.

JK: I ask you for justice.

MJ: That is not justice; you were a rubbish manager.

JK: Then someone else can suffer then, as I suffer. How much shall I pay you?

MJ: Joe… What have I ever done to make you treat me so disrespectfully? Had you come to me in friendship, then the scum would be suffering this very day while you worked for me. And that by chance if an honest man such as yourself should make enemies, then they would become my enemies. And then they would fear you.

JK: Be my friend. (Then, after bowing) Godfather?

MJ: (After Joe kisses his hand.) Some day, and that day may never come, I'll call upon you to do a service for me. But until that day, accept this justice as a gift on my daughter's big day. (A jubilant Joe leaves the room and Martin looks to Chris Hughton.) Get him a job at Highbury. Give that Wenger an offer he can't refuse.

Ricardo Moniz is sitting in the club gym when a dejected Jermain Defoe walks in.

JD: Hey, how come I been put outta my locker?

RM: Lee Barnard needed it.

JD: It took me two months to learn the combination of that locker.

RM: Ya want the truth? Ya got heart, but ya play like a bum. The only thing special about you is ya never got ya nose broke. Keep ya nose pretty and what's left of ya brain and retire.

JD: That's a bit harsh, coach. (He begins to walk off.)

RM: (Feeling bad.) Come here, kid. I guess we could all do with a second chance.

He puts on a video of Charlton's last game.

RM: Now look at that Thomas Myhre. His shot-stopping is great, can't lie 'bout that. Now you have a problem keeping onside. Doesn't look so good but we can work on that.

Jermain nods and they both watch the flickering screen.

RM: See how he plays sometimes. Drives his manager nuts. Nobody knows his next move, him included. It's all about that killer instinct and you need that killer touch. You got the power to rip the ball right past him.

They watch more action.

RM: Jermain, when you walk onto the pitch, you gonna be ready, you gonna be ready 'cause I been waiting for 20 years… 20 years to win something in England. When I'm done with you, you're gonna be able to spit nails. You're gonna be able to eat lightnin' and crap thunder. You'll be a very, very dangerous person.

Jermain, who has been staying silent and listening, nods his head. There is something different in his eyes, a new determination and hunger. He feels that the next match against Charlton might just be the turning point in his season.

Chapter Eight

February
Stuttering and Stress

Thursday February 2nd 2006

I CAN UNDERSTAND why people are so upset. The team isn't playing well, the side's ageing star defender is falling apart at the seams, the captain wants to leave, the club is behind its arch rivals and if the players keep letting the fans down the new stadium won't even be half full next season.

Anyway, enough about the freefalling Goons down the road. We're here to talk about the side currently sitting in fourth, the final Champions League place, three points and 12 goals clear of their nearest rivals. This is the same side that finished ninth the previous season and 14th the one before.

It's a team containing six England internationals and four England U21 players, not to mention the ten other internationals who ply their trade alongside them. It's certainly got talent but most of the club's fans stated at the beginning of the season that they would be quite happy with getting into the Uefa Cup.

However, something happened. The team started to pick up points, churning out wins and hard-earned points. Not only that but the players stroked the ball around as if Sir Bill was in charge and had ordered them to make sure the fans enjoyed themselves. The team shot up the table while those around them stuttered.

Stuttering and Stress

Although the results improved, the team still struggled to keep pace with some fans' lofty ambitions. Despite modest aims at the campaign's start, a section of the fans had got greedy. Rather than accepting the team was sitting higher than expected, the supporters started to act as if they frequented the Bernabeu or the Camp Nou. It was only a matter of time before the white hankies would begin to be waved.

For you see, Tottenham Hotspur had just lost their fifth game of the season. Who cared about the points gained in the other 19 games or that the team was still yet to lose two league games in a row? Who cared that all teams not bankrolled by Russian billionaires find over the course of the season that they suffer a sticky patch where chances either don't come or aren't taken?

As in previous years, a hefty slice of the fans picked a struggling striker on whom to unleash their fury. Whereas Fredi Kanoute and Mido had faced their harsh words in recent blips, now was the turn of Grzegorz Rasiak. A striker's success hinges on confidence so the fans, with all their collective Uefa coaching badges, decided the only thing to do to help the situation was to cheer the Pole ironically whenever he did something well.

He responded in kind to their brilliant tactical manoeuvre by sinking into a shell so bereft of belief that he was actually paying people to take the ball away from him whenever he received it.

Who knows what the future holds for Rasiak? Kanoute was the butt of various lazy jibes and what happened? He left and the same fans cried for his return. After a dazzling debut, Mido was slammed every week for being fat, lumbering and out of shape. He was even getting criticised this season while notching goals. Then he scored some more, picked up some praise from the media, went to the African Nations Cup, and the same fans cried for his return. How dare you use that fickle word.

Then came the transfer window – 31 days of pure, unadulterated baseless rumour and excitement. People who knew Daniel Levy's mum's hamster assured fans that this star and that bloke with the foreign sounding name would join by the end of the month. Speculation grew and grew until only the time-travelling arrival of a young Pele, Maradona or George Best on the stroke of 11.59pm on deadline day would have satisfied the gossip-crazed supporters.

"Listen to me, Martin," screamed hordes of torch-bearing, wide-eyed fans demanding a left-winger and a striker. Behind the scenes, the management team attempted to plug the obvious squad gaps but their efforts were rebuffed by clubs simply not wanting to sell in the winter window. The head coach tried to explain that the squad would only be added to over the next month if the available player was of the requisite quality.

Fringe players were shipped out for extremely good money, while two higher quality replacement internationals were brought in for less than half the money recouped. A deadline day deal to bring in someone for the left failed in the final hours, and the fans, still tending to open wounds left by a last-minute loss to Fulham, vented their anger.

"The manager is a fool!" "What's he doing?" "Has he lost the plot?" "We want Torres!" the mob shrieked at the walls of White Hart Lane. A small chanting child in the angry throng stopped in the midst of it all and turned to his father. "Dad, where are we in the league?" the youngster asked. "Fourth, son. Keep that torch up high." The little boy looked quizzically at the ground.

"Weren't we there before we lost those games, when everyone was saying how good we were?" he inquired.

"Yes, boy. Don't stop chanting," the father said before turning back to the crowd. The child stroked his chin for a moment and then tugged on his dad's arm. The huge, gorilla of a man turned once more, neck veins bulging.

"Is the squad weaker now than the one that kept us in fourth before the transfer window?" the youngster asked. His dad put his banner down and knelt beside the boy. "No son, I suppose it's better. As we couldn't get a left-winger, Mr Jol brought in a player who was not only better than the departed midfielders but could supply the ball to our strikers as well as any winger." He looked at the bellowing swarm of supporters and then back at his son.

"Let's go shall we, kiddo?" The two slipped away from the crowd and walked down Tottenham High Street. The little boy held something in his hands. It was a Spurs scarf bearing the famous cockerel crowing proudly upon its ball. The man put his arm round his son's shoulder and said: "You hold that as high as you can, boy. We're Lilywhites and you're right... it's not all doom and Goon."

Sunday February 5th 2006

FA Premiership
Tottenham Hotspur 3 Charlton 1
Attendance – 36,034
Spurs goalscorers: Defoe (2), Jenas

Thursday February 9th 2006

I JUST WATCHED Jermain Defoe's goals again from Sunday's game and I realised there is definitely one aspect of Tottenham Hotspur's past and present that we fans can look on with pride and satisfaction.

We all love them. They are the players who you pray

the ball will fall to because they are machines. Like all predators they were born to fulfil their one function on earth. Only a few of these true poachers are produced in each generation and they can be identified by that single-minded desire to see the net bulge.

"I don't know why, but I found it easy. Scoring goals came naturally to me. I never felt tension, nerves, any sort of pressure and I never lacked confidence. I'd been scoring goals regularly since I was a boy and I had it in my head that it was something I was born to do.

"I loved it alright. I used to compare it to a shooting star. Because even on the greyest winter afternoon the ball kissing the back of the net was as if a brilliant light had suddenly illuminated the ground, a moment that passed just as quickly as it had come."

Any of the Spurs goal-scoring legends could have said that. Clive Allen, my childhood hero Gary Lineker, Jürgen Klinsmann, Bobby Smith or even our current great hope, Jermain Defoe. It was in fact the man that they all peek out from the shadow of, the absurdly prolific Jimmy Greaves, writing in his autobiography *Greavsie*.

Spurs have been spoiled over the years with a plethora of poachers. Their records speak for themselves. Greaves (266 gls/379 apps), Smith (208/317), Allen (112/173), Lineker (80/138), Klinsmann (38/68) and now the early days of Jermain Defoe, who is currently on 36/85.

However poorly the rest of the team are playing, however unlikely a goal seems, the rain may be sweeping miserably across the pitch and stands but these are the players who with barely a sniff of a chance can pounce and in a microsecond have 36,000 people roaring off their seats and feeling warm inside once more.

They are arrogant yet realistic, egotistical but worthy of their own applause, they give out disgusted looks when a fellow professional blasts the ball over instead of squaring it to their clinical feet. These poachers are confident that nine times out of ten, they'll smack that ball into the net, taking the glory and confirming their attitude.

The defiant defenders and magical midfield maestros will always be popular with the fans but nothing sticks in the mind more than the moment you saw your striker place the ball past the opposition keeper. One day, they'll name a stand in either the rebuilt White Hart Lane or in a new Spurs stadium after Jimmy Greaves and it'll sound perfect.

Goalscorers make the beautiful game so pretty. Despite his ultimately disastrous Spurs career, I will always cherish the moment that Sergei Rebrov scored his first goal for the club against Everton at the Lane on September 5th 2000. We were 2-0 down and he turned the game on its head.

It was the first strike since his £11m move from Dinamo Kiev and where did he run to celebrate? Straight over to a crowd of fans to the side of the goal, including my delighted father and I, and roared his delight. Understandably, we roared back. So did his team-mates and Spurs won 3-2 with further goals from Rebrov and Les Ferdinand. There's nothing like a goalscorer.

Down at the Lane nowadays, there's a young pretender gunning for Greaves' title who has followed a remarkably similar path to his legendary predecessor. Both starred for London youth teams, Jimmy for the London Schoolboys and Jermain for SENRAB, scoring ridiculous amounts of goals.

Both had a habit of scoring on their club debuts throughout their careers. The strikers suffered equal disillusionment at their initial capital clubs with Greaves tiring of Chelsea's inconsistencies in the old

First Division while Defoe was disgusted at West Ham's relegation in 2003.

Each was on the receiving end of some poor advice from those around them. Greavsie with debt-ridden Chelsea officials persuading him to spend an ill-fated adventure with AC Milan and the current youngster with a lack of guidance that saw a poorly received transfer request the day after the Hammers were plunged into obscurity and an earlier highly publicised transfer from his first club Charlton to West Ham.

Both errors were Spurs' gain with £99,999 and £7m transfers respectively. Along with spells at West Ham, the two matchwinners now share one club, the glory-soaked Tottenham Hotspur, as their spiritual home. That's where the difference occurs. Whereas Jimmy came at a time when things could not get much better for the double-winning Spurs side, Jermain has come into a team beginning to rediscover its glorious past.

Another happy difference is that unlike players from Jimmy's generation, Defoe is a young man who is far happier sitting in front of endless televised matches and highlights, studying fellow strikers, than going out for a beer with the lads. That culture should help him steer clear of the problems that hampered the end of Jimmy's career and subsequent years.

The Spurs fans have taken to Defoe as they did in 1962 to his then young counterpart, although there will always be the few that won't respect his talent. It remains to be seen whether his international manager falls into that camp, but the signs aren't good.

There's always the fear that his talent and ambition will see him fly the nest if he's kept on the bench for another lengthy spell. Rather than fearing the worst, how about believing that conversely his talent will galvanise the squad and drag it with him into the stratosphere? If he is to stamp his mark on the club's colourful history, with future youngsters being compared to him, then he must be given the opportunity to do what he does best. Get on the pitch, score goals and lots of them.

Greaves scored 44 goals in 57 appearances for England, a better ratio than Bobby Charlton, the all-time top scorer. It's early days for Defoe in that department but if he gets the chances the signs are that he can emulate his fellow striker. Hopefully he won't be left out in 2006 in the way that Greavsie was so cruelly, 40 years previously.

However old you are, you'll have a goalscorer who you hold close to your heart at Tottenham Hotspur. Most other clubs can only drool at our rich vein of lethal finishers. Let's hope that our latest instalment keeps them and us salivating for years to come.

Jimmy Greaves made a crashing impact on British football with his grace, speed and lethal finishing and during the 1960s it was a common cry among boys across the country when a goal was smashed in a playground football match: "Who do you think you are, Jimmy Greaves?" Let's hope that we finally have someone who can eventually proclaim: "No, I'm better."

Sunday February 12th 2006

FA Premiership
Sunderland 1 Tottenham Hotspur 1
Attendance – 34,700
Spurs goalscorer: Keane

Thursday February 16th 2006

WITH SECONDS LEFT on the clock and the double-footed lunges of both Cesc Fabregas and Matthieu Flamini flying towards him, Michael Carrick performed a remarkable Zidanesque pirouette between the youngsters.

As they crashed into each other, he looked up briefly and chipped the ball over the back-peddalling Jens Lehmann who ended up tangled and weeping in the net. The game was won and as Carrick was mobbed by team-mates he pointed to one man in the dugout and grinned.

That will be Saturday April 22nd 2006, but the foundations for the goal were laid on September 29th 2005 when Ricardo Moniz arrived at White Hart Lane from PSV Eindhoven. He came with a big reputation across Europe as one of the few protégés of the Dutch training guru Will Coerver. Through Coerver's methods, the Portuguese trainer would be bringing with him a technique of breaking down and drilling the greatest stars' touches, controls and moves into any player.

Along with an Olympic diving instructor, he had worked closely with PSV youngsters such as Arjen Robben as they developed through the academy. Lilywhite fans began to salivate with images of Goran Bunjevcevic performing a Hugo Sanchez overhead kick or Johnnie Jackson running the length of the pitch bouncing the ball on his head à la Ronaldinho. Every Saturday morning would surely see Soccer AM's showboat montage dedicated to Tottenham Hotspur.

Lee Young-Pyo studied under the Portugeezer at PSV and there's little doubt he can take on and dribble past any player in his way. Unfortunately, the diminutive South Korean missed one session under Moniz. While suffering from the after effects of a dodgy spring roll, Lee was forced to sit out one sunny September day when the coach helped the club's players strengthen their weaker feet.

Moniz's brief when he joined Tottenham Hotspur was to introduce progressively the 94 tricks he knows inside out into the games of all the players at the club – ranging from the numerous youth sides to the first team. More importantly, in a one-footed Premiership, it was part of his job description to help produce future generations of two-footed Lilywhites. What a scary thought. No need to scream up at the stadium walls for a left-winger every transfer window. What will we do?

In training ground photos, you often see him in the background with a small group of players seemingly going over various techniques. While it's not part of his repertoire to teach players to stop conceding late goals, the fruits of his five months worth of labour so far do seem to have started to creep into individual performances in recent weeks. I may be wrong, but Michael Carrick in particular seems to have added a number of space-making tricks to his game.

While he always had the ability to use the ball well in pressured situations, the long-sleeved midfielder now seems to have gained extra time with an ability to jink in and out of challenges, twisting and turning, culminating in a superb move during the Charlton game – not entirely dissimilar to the dream one in the introduction – which left two opponents sprawled on the floor.

Another man who looks to have benefited from the new trainer is Paul Stalteri. Although much maligned for his Paris Hiltonesque shielding of the ball from Daryl Murphy last weekend, he seems to have gained more confidence on the ball as the season has gone on. In his first few months, he was more likely to perform an Anthony 'Bambi in the headlights' Gardner lump away rather than taking on a man or taking time to find a pass. Still far from the perfect attacking wing-back, he does link up well with either Jenas or Lennon ahead of him. His crossing and passing has improved no end and his goal against Leicester marked that new confidence although it will be lost in the mire of that horrible defeat.

The whole squad seems more confident on the ball. The youngsters like Dawson and Lennon are clearly benefiting from the ability to make space and time for themselves. From his handful of performances in the last month, Huddlestone is showing skills when in possession that certainly weren't as evident in the Derby or England U21 games I caught last season. Like Carrick he had composure but not the fast feet. Whether the new-found skills are from Moniz or Hoddle remains to be seen though.

The main thing that the trainer's 94 tricks bring to the side's play is the ability to keep possession. While the final killer pass isn't always part of our play, we stroke the ball about better than most teams in the Premiership. Jamie Carragher recently commented that Liverpool players were saying in the dressing room after our visit, that Spurs were possibly the hardest team from England or Europe they'd played at Anfield this season.

He admitted that at times, even as the home side, they just couldn't get the ball off us. It's that unflustered use of the ball that has come with a blend of Moniz's work, Jol's ethos and Davids' experience and influence. Obviously it can be argued that other influences have also made a difference to our play but aspects of the new skill coach's work must be playing some part.

In contrast to last season, how many sides have been able to hurry and fluster our players into conceding possession? How many sides have actually beaten us for possession this season compared to last? It's a difference that has proved a big boost away from White Hart Lane in relation to last year.

As The Pitbull has pointed out this week, possession doesn't win games, but it certainly lays the foundations for success. If ever we wanted someone to help Jol bring back the style and panache of Sir Bill's days, Moniz is the man. All the sides previously considered as the 'big four' are or were masters at stroking the ball around and eating away at their opponents mentally. That's where Spurs are heading.

Tottenham Hotspur of old was a side laced with flashes of skill but no backbone. I'm excited about the future. With Ricardo and the confidence he will bring in players' own abilities, I want to see Spurs break into that quartet fusing strength and skill with a healthy dose of Jol's winning mentality.

Sunday February 19th 2006

FA Premiership
Tottenham Hotspur 2 Wigan 2
Attendance – 35,676
Spurs goalscorers – Mido, Defoe

Chapter Nine

March
Crowing Lions

Thursday March 3rd 2006

IN THE 68th minute of England's World Cup warm up game against South American opposition, Tottenham Hotspur finally got a man on the pitch.

That man was Teddy Sheringham, Spurs' sole representative among the 23 players on the pitch and the packed bench. The psychics among the crowd could argue that Danny Murphy came on 23 minutes beforehand, but that's just silly. The date was April 17th 2002 and the South American side was actually our World Cup opponents this year, Paraguay.

It's proof of how far we've come in the national set-up. Even Arsène himself couldn't fail to spot that England finished their latest game on Wednesday night with five Spurs players on the pitch. It was a proud night for the club and was the first time a quintet of Lilywhites had taken over the national side in 18 years.

I wouldn't dare say that we won the game once those players were on the pitch or that the side looked pretty good once they had taken over. Oops, I just did. The papers the next day were singing the praises of Michael Carrick and rightly so. The cultured midfielder put in a performance so laid back, his mullet was touching the grass for most of the game. We all knew he was the answer to the holding midfielder role and finally Sven saw sense.

The fact that he saw him as the instant choice to replace Lampard hopefully means that Michael can start fumbling around in his wardrobe for his summer lederhosen. That's unless Sven failed to spot that both goals started from the long-sleeved one's inch-perfect passes to Joe Cole and then Shaun Wright-Phillips. Considering the bespectacled Lothario's comments after the game that thankfully doesn't seem to be the case.

Standing between the sticks was the guardian of the nation. The man whose job it is to single-handedly stop other countries scoring while assassinating England team-mates who are blocking Spurs players from the team or have turned down a move to Tottenham in the past. Rumour has it that Lampard's injury came about after Robinson ran the length of the training pitch to do the crane kick from *The Karate Kid* on the Chelsea player.

Jermaine Jenas and Ledley King came on at half-time to double the Tottenham quotient. While Jenas resumed his partnership with Carrick for the national side, King slotted in alongside Rio "I'm so calm, I'm so cool... oops" Ferdinand. The difference between the two was obvious as King used the ball intelligently and calmly and Ferdinand made sure he was tackled enough times for the photographers to catch the moment.

King is certain to board the plane to Germany due to his versatility and, quite frankly, his brilliance. Jenas is a little less assured of a ticket, but if he keeps steadily improving at Tottenham then I can't see many able to push him out of the squad. The attacking midfielder, like King, brings Sven's much-loved versatility tag to the table as he can play pretty much anywhere across the middle and can score goals.

Competition wise, the pundits have an unhealthy obsession with Scott Parker but Svenny boy seems to disagree. Kevin Nolan may yet force himself in through brute force and goals, but the Swede in charge is apparently "unaware of that Bolton place". Jenas holds the cards because he's playing in a team currently higher up the table, is one of Sven's favourites if the rumours of Levy bidding for him on the Swede's advice are true, and he has the international experience under his belt to take to a major tournament.

The final bit of the five-pieced jigsaw is Jermain Defoe. Initially I was extremely unhappy that the diminutive poacher had been given only his usual 10 minutes or so from Sven to impress. I wailed and moaned at everyone who would listen that this was ridiculously unfair. To me, Jermain has the potential to be the Toto Schillaci of this World Cup. A man who isn't particularly well known to international defences and comes into a team through injury and ends up becoming a star.

Then I sat down and thought about it and common sense prevailed. I realised that Sven knows all about Jermain with his season ticket to the Lane. His assistant, Tord, certainly has a very high opinion of Defoe and has frequently said in the past that he is England's next Michael Owen. I think the reasoning behind Darren Bent's 80 minutes or so was that Sven wanted to take a fair last look at the Charlton striker to see whether he could nick into the squad.

The answer was there for all to see. While Bent was energetic and enthusiastic with his running, I don't think he broke into double figures with touches of the ball. He found, as many do, that international defences are a different beast to those of the Premiership. I was listening to radio commentary for some of the first half as I was driving home and even they were joking about Bent setting a new record for watching a game rather than playing it.

Crowing Lions

He's a decent enough player but did anyone else wonder why Graeme Le Saux kept proclaiming with each play that Bent had "moved brilliantly and timed his run perfectly" despite the fact that replays showed quite clearly that the striker was almost in the stands by the time the ball was passed.

I also wondered whether Sven is actually training Jermain up to be an impact sub with different qualities to Peter Crouch. He still got that 10 minutes at the end despite the fact that there was a Champions League player left on the pitch in Joe Cole. Sven still wanted Defoe on although Wayne Bridge's injury meant he would have to break his reported promise to rest all the Chelski and Liverpool players in some way. I reckon that as long as Defoe features regularly enough in the run-in, he's going to make the squad. With his time on the bench in the middle of the season, he will also bring a freshness with him to the tournament that others won't.

Away from England for a second, it was great news first to see Robbie Keane get the Ireland captaincy, second to score a lovely volley and then third sign a new four-year deal today.

While I was initially sceptical of the impact the Irishman would have this season, he's been superb for the majority of his games. He's also grown as a leader rather than the moaning whinger he was at times last year. That will only continue with his new national responsibility.

With our internationals and our batch of U21s things are looking healthy for Tottenham Hotspur's domination of international football. That's for the future though as our thoughts turn to their return to White Hart Lane on Sunday. I want to see some proud Cockerels strutting their stuff on the pitch after a couple of slip-ups. First Europe, lads, then the world.

Sunday March 5th 2006

FA Premiership
Tottenham Hotspur 3 Blackburn 2
Attendance – 36,080
Spurs goalscorers – Keane (2), Mido

WHO NEEDS STRESS in your work or private life when you support Tottenham Hotspur? Today Blackburn came and saw and were conquered by a mugger known as Robbie Keane. I suffered six minor heart attacks at different points in the game and at one point kicked the corner of a seat in annoyance and stupidity and had to fight back the tears for the next half an hour.

Ten minutes into the action and I thought we were flying. The Irishman currently celebrating the best week of his young life had scored a goal so cheeky and brilliant that White Hart Lane practically burst at the seams as the ball hit the net.

Not only did he flick the ball impudently past two Blackburn players before lashing it past Brad 'Hellboy' Friedel, but one of the victims of his outrageous skill was The Most Unlikely Premiership Footballer Ever™, Robbie Savage. Is there any better sight in football than the Welshman choking on his flowing locks as he watches yet another better player get past him?

From then on, however, it was all Blackburn. The term 'against the run of play' was invented for goals like our second and third. At one point I could have sworn I saw Michael Dawson and Ledley King putting on tin hats and standing barricaded inside our penalty area. Our captain was distressingly torn from side to side by the B Grade Premiership strike force of Craig Bellamy and Florent Sinama Pongolle.

You could almost sense his relief when he got the more

traditional, burly Shefki Kuqi to battle with towards the end of the game. The pacey, fleet-footed strikers pulled King all over the place and Dawson was often caught out of position trying to cover for him. The new Spurs technique of lumping the ball forward towards Mido at every opportunity hardly helped the defence's cause.

Ever since the target man returned from calling coaches "donkeys" in Africa, the instructions have been to arrow the ball at him from every area of the pitch. This results in 90 per cent of the balls falling back to the opposition's feet. Whereas White Hart Lane was a chance-making haven for the team pre-January, our reliance on the Egyptian has seen us dominated by Wigan and Blackburn in successive home games.

Thank goodness for Robbie. Had he not produced his moment of magic when nobody would support him, bundled the ball basketball-style past Friedel and then released Aaron Lennon to cross for Mido, we would not currently be sitting five points clear of our nearest rivals, some lesser team from North London.

I felt bad for Jermain Defoe, who started on the bench despite three goals in three games before today. However, Jol's selection was repaid and then some with a superb performance from the Irish captain. While I think Defoe is a legend of the future, when Robbie's on song he can blow apart any opposition defence.

Davids was sharper than he has been in previous weeks but faded badly as the game went on, probably due to his recent injury. Jenas also had one of his more anonymous games, which was surprising after his decent half for England in the week. He seemed to display a tendency to knock the ball back as soon as he got it, much to the annoyance of the White Hart Lane faithful.

Tainio was his usual combative self but was also

suffering from a lack of match fitness as the game wore on. When Murphy replaced him late in the match, we seemed to calm down again with the new signing's measured passes and control of the ball.

At the back, Blackburn played on Lee's obvious lack of height and battered him with Stephen Reid's physical presence throughout the second half. The left-back is still settling into the hustle and bustle of the Premiership and his reliance on his right foot must cause slightly embarrassing moments in the Lee household when he watches *Match of the Day* in the evenings.

Talking of television coverage, what is the deal with Alan Pardew being paid handsomely to act as a pundit for our recent games? What connection does he have with either us or our opposition?

The man couldn't be more biased if he turned up with a West Ham scarf and hat, waving a banner proclaiming "We want a draw!" He has issues with former West Ham players having left for better things at Tottenham. Against Wigan a fortnight ago, he told the viewers he was disappointed with Jermain and how he was performing nowadays despite the striker equalising for Spurs.

Yeah right, Alan. I can see Bobby Zamora and Marlon Harewood pushing into England's World Cup squad over the diminutive hitman. Sour grapes over losing a player is a very sad thing to watch on national television. I find it very strange that a man who was on the verge of being sacked not so long ago has become so smug so quickly.

It seems like only yesterday his fans would boo him from the terraces every week after each successive loss or bore draw. Now in his first Premiership season, he's already mouthing off to Sky's Richard Keys about how he hopes to turn over Spurs on the last game of the campaign especially if "it means something". One swan does not a Hammer make, Alan.

I'm hoping that to have won a match when our overall performance was so wretched will see the end of this slump. What better way to come out of the mire than to put in a glory glory show against the Champions at Red Square? A new pitch has been laid at Stamford Beach and it could be just the surface for Spurs to start playing their way into Europe again.

We've got a lot of big games coming up and as Mido put in a typically footballer-clichéd way this week, "every one is a cup final". Only four of our remaining ten matches are at White Hart Lane. Among the six away games are trips to Chelsea, a rejuvenated Newcastle and the Goons while two of our home games are against Manchester United and Bolton. It's not all doom and gloom as our closest rivals from down the road still have to play Liverpool, Manchester United and us as well as making up the five points on us.

It's going to be tough but if we want to get into the Champions League we have to start playing like champions.

Saturday March 11th 2006

FA Premiership
Chelsea 2 Tottenham Hotspur 1
Attendance – 42,243
Spurs goalscorer – Jenas

Sunday March 12th 2006

I DON'T KNOW what's worse – expecting to lose and seeing that happen or being given hope and watching that crushed in the dying seconds. The first is definitely not my style, which means I have to suffer the painful effects of the latter.

This season that has meant crushing blows to the heart and senses against Grimsby, West Ham, Leicester, Fulham, Sunderland and now Chelsea. Conceding last-minute goals against that many teams is as ridiculous as it is stupid. Every season contains the odd injury-time heartbreaker but to have six just shows poor organisation and concentration.

Had we held firm in those games we would be six points better off and still in both cup competitions. With the extra points and fewer goals against, we would currently be sitting in third ahead of Liverpool on goal difference – a clear nine points above the Champions League qualification line.

It's as frustrating as it is disappointing. The excuses will be churned out, reminding everyone that it's a young team that will grow with the experience. True, they are young, but there's enough experience on the pitch to tell the young ones to either keep the line or stop walloping the ball back to the opposition. One of those experienced league winners is Paul Stalteri who was culpable for his poor clearance in the dying moments that fell softly to Damien Duff, who in turn laid it off for Gallas to strike his killer blow.

Fair play to the Frenchman. It was a tremendous hit and would have beaten any keeper in the world, as it did England's Number One who had valiantly kept out so many preceding Chelsea strikes, including a point-blank Drogba volley. However, the left-back should not have been allowed to get into that position, drifting past two limp-lettuce challenges before unleashing the shot into the corner.

Things had pretty much gone to plan before that moment barring an unusually nervous performance from Michael Carrick. With Sven watching from the stands, the long-sleeved midfielder gave the ball away on countless occasions and looked uneasy as he was closed down by Chelsea's midfield. It was his loose pass across the face of his own penalty area that put Shaun Wright-Phillips through to cut back for a Michael Essien mis-hit into the corner.

His corners must also rank down there as some of the worst in the Premiership. He seems to think playing a high and drifting ball to the back of the penalty area is the way to success. If by success he means watching the ball being smacked out of the area or the keeper grabbing it and starting up a dangerous breakaway then congratulations, job done. The enormous contrast with Lampard's corners in yesterday's game, and Beckham's for England last week, should have shown the willowy wizard that goals come from balls whipped into the six-yard area.

In contrast to Carrick's performance, the more experienced Tainio and Davids played superbly keeping the Chelsea hordes at bay. While the latter was back to his combative Pitbull best, the former's grit and constant flicks to Lee on the left were a great outlet to break up the blue-shirted attacks.

The little Korean was another positive to take from the rubble of the defeat. He had one of his best games defensively since he signed. How he relished playing someone smaller than him in Wright-Phillips for a change. No being clobbered as he went for headers or being thrown into the sidelines by rampaging six-footers. When faced with someone with genuine pace and trickery, Lee coped very well and was rarely beaten by the England winger.

Jermaine Jenas on the other side had a strange game. He seemed to appear in fits and bursts throughout the match. He was largely anonymous in the first half until he made a perfectly timed run onto Dawson's header to dink the ball over the onrushing Petr Cech. In the second half, with the confidence from the goal, he was more involved and chased back on a number of occasions to win the ball. He should have scored a second and possibly wrapped up the game when Ledley King put him through with a terrific pitch-long pass. However, his four-year-old girl's shot bobbled softly into Cech's hands.

Clever old Jose had also anticipated our brilliantly devious tactic of knocking a long ball up to Mido's head every couple of seconds. The Egyptian was always closely marked by Robert Huth or John Terry who are no slouches in the air themselves. Talking of the long-haired Spurs striker, whether he or Jol came up with the fantastic idea of him playing on the left-wing, trying to cross into the empty space where he should have been – it was a stroke of genius. While Mido's ability in the air is unquestioned, he has the explosive pace of my grandmother and an ability to fall over his own feet at the exact moment he looks to cross.

All in all, though, we made the champions look very ordinary. They had a few decent chances but in the end we did enough to take home a point or even nick a win. For the first 15 minutes of the game and almost all of the second half, we more than matched Chelsea across the Stamford Bridge pitch. It was the same at White Hart Lane earlier in the season, until Rob Styles pulled on his blue shirt and sent off Mido for jumping in the air.

Despite all that, we trudged home on both occasions without any points. The heartbreak for all the players was personified in the magnificent Michael Dawson as he collapsed to the floor with his head in his hands as Gallas' once-in-a-lifetime shot nestled in the net. We have experienced a reversal of Blackburn's fortunes, who played well against us last week but lost, and were truly awful against Aston Villa yesterday yet won. For us, we deserved to get hammered by Blackburn but won and played far better against the might of Chelsea yet lost. Football, eh?

The question now is: will we suffer a hangover from this painful defeat or will we let our other opponents experience a serious backlash? Champions League football is still in our grasp as long as we don't let our heads drop. A win at struggling Birmingham is a must next week if we are to get back on track and restore confidence. We have to pick up points in our easier games.

Talking of struggling teams, hats off to our old Portugeezer Pedro Mendes who scored two long-range goals right out of the top drawer for relegation battlers Portsmouth. I still remember his cracking goal against Everton last season as if it was yesterday and of course *The Night When Pedro Did What Pele Couldn't* ™.

His long-range shots against Manchester City to seal a last-minute win at Fratton Park yesterday showcased the tremendous technique of the Champions League winner. It was a shame to see him go and despite the queue in front of him, he never complained or attacked the club when he left as others have. All the best to you, Pedro, keep winding up that right boot and shooting and also, look after young Wayne for us, will you?

Saturday March 18th 2006

FA Premiership
Birmingham 0 Tottenham Hotspur 2
Attendance – 26,398
Spurs goalscorers – Lennon, Keane

Sunday March 19th 2006

I LOOKED AT my hand during the first half yesterday and it was shaking. Not in a *One Flew Over the Cuckoo's Nest* style act of slowly crumbling sanity, but because my whole body was full to the brim with nervous excitement.

In years gone by, with the run-in meaning the difference between 14th and 9th place, we would have expected to wallop a struggling Birmingham team and probably would have. But this weekend, we were playing a Birmingham side fighting for its Premiership survival with a dangerous 12th man on their side – pressure.

With every team except West Ham's reserves winning around us, we simply had to win. For two hours, those Ribena-shirted types from down the road were actually above us. It's a rare thing for Lilywhites to bear that much pressure on their shoulders, but that's what this last slew of matches are going to be all about. They don't call it the business end of the season for nothing.

For 45 minutes, I wasn't sure whether we'd be able to cope. The boys looked nervous and Carrick and Jenas were both giving the ball away as if it was smeared in something rather unsavoury. The team did their transfixed rabbit act as the Brum players followed the age-old 'hassle Tottenham' formula. In their terror, the Spurs players pinged the ball up to the head of Mido. Unfortunately, they soon realised the Egyptian was on the bench and in his place up front was the rather smaller Jermain Defoe.

Paul Stalteri lost his place for his part in a number of recent last-minute horror shows. Stephen Kelly came in and had a solid game, keeping up easily with the ageing legs of Stan Lazaridis. The supersonic Oompa Loompa also came in for his first start in a while on the right.

How we've missed his jinking runs in recent weeks and how he was going to repay Jol for his inclusion.

After the nerve-strewn first half ended with Robbie Keane being tackled by Mario Melchiot, seconds from converting Jenas' superb ball across the six-yard box, the boys must have sat in the dressing room playing computer games, listening to iPods or doing whatever they do to calm down, because the team that emerged for the second half at St Andrews was the one that got us into our position in the first place.

They stroked the ball about as if they were at White Hart Lane. The Birmingham resistance ebbed away until finally Jermain made the breakthrough in front of the frosted spectacles of Sven Goran Eriksson. As Melchiot confidently shepherded a ball towards the touchline, Defoe sprinted up to him and nicked the ball. In his fury, the looming Dutch giant fell towards the diminutive thief and grabbed his ankle as he tried to escape with his magic beans.

Showing off increased strength on the ball – surely what he's been working on during his spare bench time – he shrugged off the giant's hand and sprinted past Kenny Cunningham before whipping the ball into the box. Jenas performed a brilliant dummy, which many would have seen as a totally foolish-looking miss, and the ball fell to Lennon. I screamed at the little winger as the ball stuck under his right foot.

He dismissed my ignorant cries with a flick of the foot and cut inside onto his left and curled the ball into the corner of the net. I screamed in a display of joy unseen since my father realised that his dribbling one-year-old had just said the word "Spurs". I still dribble and shout the same word. How ironic.

The pressure was off. Even the fear of a last-minute equaliser seemed distant as the Birmingham players' resistance was broken. Even the fans turned on Melchiot for an unfortunate mistake that many a footballer will make in his career. The threat of MC Heskey and DJ Campbell was blunted, probably because the former had been injured and replaced by Mikael Forssell.

It was only a matter of time before the second goal came along to totally flatten them. Another terrific burst of speed from Jenas took him to the edge of the area and, as he did in the first half, he played an inch-perfect ball across to Keane and this time the Irish captain stroked the ball home. It was a case of job done – not the greatest performance in the world, but with the added pressure a professional one.

The man of the match was undoubtedly Michael Dawson. How much longer can Sven ignore the claims of the best young defender in the country? If this rumoured England B international comes about in May, the Swede could do a lot worse than give the oak-hearted kid a chance. His all-action, 'screw the danger' style is very reminiscent of John Terry and with each passing game his reading of the play grows. Playing alongside the King is shaping a kid with a lot of potential into something very special.

For a team so young, to have even got this far and still be in fourth place is a major achievement. I was asked today whether I'd take fifth place now or risk losing the chance of European football, whatever form it may arrive in. Obviously at the start of the season, I would have bitten off the hand of anyone willing to offer such a deal. Now, I'm just not sure any more.

Martin and his Jolly Babies have installed in me a terrifying optimism that despite an equally terrifying run of games, and the chance that I may lose my sanity along the way, we might just be able to make it. Hell, we're already at our points total for last season and we still have eight games to go. The improvement is there for all to see, so why can't we make that last step? It's ahead of schedule but it's no more than our youngsters deserve. The French Foreign Legion certainly don't have any more right to it than we do.

The nerves will all return next Monday as we play pretty much exactly the same type of game again. A game we should win against struggling relegation candidates but fortunately this time, we of the White Hart Lane faithful will be there to cheer the lads on. Once again all the other games will have been played by the time our game rolls around on Monday and there is a chance that once again we may have to reclaim our position, unless our old friends at Portsmouth can do us some favours.

We have to be wary of the Baggies, as the same match in the run-in last year produced an extremely lame 1-1 draw, and obviously who could forget the even more pathetic performance in December? The warning signs are all there, but if Saturday's effort was anything to go by then the boys would seem to have the stomach for the fight.

I read this week that Aaron Lennon turned down the chance to represent the Republic of Ireland after talking to Steve Staunton and Robbie Keane. Can you tap someone up for a national side? I wonder how Sven felt. He must have been raging within his iceman exterior. Only a couple of months ago, he was saying that certain players, and he included Lennon in a shortlist, had an outside chance of forcing their way into the World Cup squad.

I don't think the youngster has played enough to sneak into the set-up that quickly but he'll be involved sooner rather than later. Fair play to him for recognising that fact rather than taking the quick fix easy way out that many footballers seem to snatch nowadays because their grandmother's dog was born in another country. Lennon would be an instant choice for Ireland's right wing now.

However, at 18, and with David Beckham's international career going to come to a close in the next few years, Lennon could grab his spot on the England wing and move onto a whole other level. This looks increasingly likely as long as Shaun Wright-Phillips' career stutters as his bank balance grows at Chelski.

What better time for him to prove his worth to Spurs and Sven than in this, the mother of all run-ins? Give us some more sparkling displays against the likes of West Brom, Manchester United, Arsenal and Bolton and I'll personally carry you to Germany in the summer, Aaron, whether Sven wants you there or not.

Monday March 27th 2006

FA Premiership
Tottenham Hotspur 2 West Brom 1
Attendance – 36,152
Spurs goalscorer – Keane (2)

Tuesday March 28th 2006

THEY SAY THAT sometimes you get what you deserve in life, while others say that football is life. Tomasz Kuszczak finds himself this morning wedged painfully between the two sayings.

The Polish 'keeper spent around 70 minutes taunting the White Hart Lane crowd with the most ridiculous time-wasting seen since Damien Comolli visited Derby to sign a certain leaden-footed striker. From Curtis Davies' early goal onwards, every time the ball went out for a goal kick, Kuszczak would go through a two-minute routine.

He'd pick up the ball, look it over, checking for holes or anything that would take a bit of time to sort out. He'd get his mobile out, call his friends back home while making sure that each blade of grass was at the required height. On occasions, he was aided by dumb Spurs fans who felt the need to throw things onto the pitch around him. That'll speed up proceedings, boys.

With his antics, that bizarrely warranted at least three final warnings from the referee, he probably wasted a good seven to eight minutes of the game. I reckoned he'd have walked naked through the White Hart Lane faithful if it meant getting them back for his team to equalise after his almighty last-minute cock-up.

It was as if the gods were gritting their teeth with each posture and pose emanating from the attention-loving Pole. The one with his finger on the trigger was being told by the others "wait… wait… now!" With the ball at his feet for a simple clearance, cool old Tomasz thought he was composed enough to dwell on the ball. Enter stage left Jermain Defoe, propelled by a lungful of breath from the gods, his determined sliding tackle blocking the clearance.

It bounced up, hit the stunned Pole on the face and looped over him. Quick as a flash of Lilywhite lightning, Defoe was off the floor and sprinting around the struggling keeper. Seeing the ball at the young England striker's feet, Kuszczak made the brilliant decision to hold onto Defoe's arm before falling on him in a final desperate, clumsy act. Robbie Keane tucked away the resulting penalty, somersaulted and finished by flicking on a big pink neon sign above the goalkeeper's head that read 'Cheats Never Prosper'.

The rest of the game had been as jam-packed with tension as I fear the rest of this run-in will be. I'm not sure if my heart will take much more. A late-night meeting at work meant I not only had to watch the game on TV but also gnash my teeth as I was forced to listen to the first fifteen minutes on my car radio on the way home. I hadn't missed much and my arrival only brought with it West Brom's sucker punch goal.

The rest is history now but I'm not ashamed to admit that when the ref ruled out Mido's goal because he'd already blown for the penalty I was actually rolling on my carpet like a fool. I'd slipped to my knees from the sofa as Defoe was brought down and then the realisation that it all depended on Robbie Keane's penalty was too much and I went down in flamboyant Didier Drogba style to the floor. I watched the penalty through my fingers before jumping up again and punching the air in exhilaration. Probably best I wasn't at White Hart Lane. I'd probably be writing this with a crayon from a padded cell.

As for the performances of the players, some were great and some were rotten. Everyone improved after Jol fixed the balance of the side after half an hour. However, my focus has to fall on Michael Carrick, who seems to have caught Robbie Savage-itis from the Chelsea game. Since that errant pass to Shaun Wright-Phillips, he seems to have dropped a couple of levels in confidence and performance. Maybe comparisons with the girly-haired Welshman are too harsh but I reckon he put in his worst shift this season last night. Passes were either going astray or backwards; the one decent pass he pulled out of the bag was the one that set up Robbie for his fantastic first chipped goal.

Perhaps it's because he set the bar so high with his consistency during the rest of the season that it's more obvious when he has a bad game. I hate to keep leaping on Carrick's back about his set-pieces but he just doesn't seem to be getting it. Every time he floats in another slow, high corner or free kick, the fans watch as it billows in the breeze. Then the groans are expelled as it's headed away by a defender who quite obviously has the momentum and advantage with such a slow, unthreatening ball. Please Michael, just whip one in.

In complete contrast, the Duracell bunny Jermaine Jenas had a cracking game. He played in central midfield, on the wing and eventually at right-back. It was an all-action performance and he looked at home in every position. They say the best footballers can play anywhere and I think people often forget JJ is still only 23. He's come on leaps and bounds this season and he's nowhere near his prime yet.

Up front Keane and Defoe toiled hard together. While the Irishman will get the plaudits for his wonderful composure and goals, his strike partner shouldn't be overlooked for his contribution and running over the whole 93 minutes.

Davids didn't look at his best although he still managed to get some vital tackles in. I think a lot of people are anticipating his tenth yellow card which will rule him out of two games. Perhaps it's been wedged in the back of the Dutchman's mind recently and affected his performances.

To be honest, he probably should have got the card against Chelsea and then could have sat out the last two 'easier' games. Now he could end up missing one or two of our games against Manchester United, Arsenal or Bolton when we need The Pitbull to be there and at his best.

Lennon was his usually dangerous self, especially when he switched to the left. One run past a couple of staring West Brom players almost resulted in a wonderful individual goal. Behind him the defence were generally untroubled apart from some bruising lone striker play from Nathan Ellington and the loss of Curtis Davies for the goal.

It was surprisingly the normally superb Michael Dawson who totally lost the West Brom centre-back in the action surrounding Jonathan Greening's free kick. To be fair to the future England international, he did seem to have two Baggies players to deal with.

At the end of the day, we stole the three points in the dying minutes and the gap has returned between us and the chasing pack. Bolton's loss and Arsenal's rained-off game helped us enormously. Further brilliant news came today with Dawson and Lennon signing new deals until 2011 and 2010 respectively. Not only have we secured the futures of two of the country's most exciting talents but it firmly puts to rest the rumours of homesickness and a move to Manchester United for the young Lennon.

The only blot on the horizon is the fact that somehow those gits down the road won again in Europe. Why oh why are the best teams in the world saving their crappest games for the Gooners? I'm starting to think it's all part of a terrifying *X-Files* style conspiracy. First Real Madrid and now Juventus have spent 90 minutes giving the ball away to Arsenal players almost as if they'd been paid to.

If that bloody lot end up winning the competition and we finish in fourth I may just spontaneously combust in the middle of the Library. To lose the Champions League place in such a way would be the biggest kick in the nuts since a certain Judas slithered down the road.

Chapter Ten

April
Squeaky Bum Time

Saturday April 1st 2006

FA Premiership
Newcastle United 3 Tottenham Hotspur 1
Attendance – 52,301
Spurs goalscorer – Keane

Wednesday April 5th 2006

I THOUGHT APRIL Fools were supposed to disappear at midday, but this year they stayed out until well after 5pm. I think we quite possibly played our worst half this season at the weekend.

On a day when we needed to race out of the traps like a greyhound, we limped out like a blind snail with a dodgy hip. As soon as I heard that Ledley King had been ruled out with a training ground ankle injury, I was filled with dread. Only one man could possibly be brought in to fill the King-sized void. Enter Anthony Gardner from stage left only to trip over.

There's no doubting that at some point, Peter Crouch's long lost half-brother grabbed the attention of scouts visiting Port Vale. However, as the years have passed below him so he seems to have, barring the odd decent game, totally lost his confidence and ability at the top level. A perfect example of why I experience the terror I do when Big Tony steps into the breach was when a 20-pass Spurs move saw the ball rolled back to the central defender. He stared at it in horror and was unsure what to do with this ball at his feet. His only option was to hammer it six feet to his right into the path of Alan Shearer.

If I were feeling like being fair to the guy I could say that he might not be sharp as he only plays once in a blue moon. Perhaps he'll prove me wrong one day if he gets a fresh start somewhere else, like Luke Young did. At the moment, though, I wouldn't put him at the back ahead of Tom Huddlestone, Noureddine Naybet and probably even the inexperienced Calum Davenport. That's how scared I get when Tony enters the fray.

Then again, there were enough similarly rubbish performances for the 7ft 9ins player to crouch down behind and hide. At least he had the excuse of not being match sharp. I don't think any of his team-mates could say they were truly at the races. The only ones who may not have got a spanking from Martin Jol after the game would possibly be Aaron Lennon and Robbie Keane, who is in the form of his life at the moment.

Finally, the Irishman seems to have found his role. I've always said that Keano is not a true striker. For me, he is more effective as a creative, skilful attacking midfielder in the Paul Scholes mould who can play just behind the main striker or even behind a pair of strikers if attack is your dish of the day. For a man who is generally considered to not be the best finisher or likeliest winner of one-on-ones with keepers, he has been hitting the back of the net regularly. He sits deep and creates, always looking to get a return pass.

I must stop waxing lyrical about Robbie as it's only deflecting the abject performance of the team. Any side that can make Lee 'I'll kill your grandmother' Bowyer look good has indeed had a very bad day at the office. Not only was he allowed to ghost in for a goal before most of us had even settled in our seats, but Edgar Davids pushing him over in the box was like waiting for the *Titanic* to sink. He was going nowhere, yet as soon as the dreadlocks started whirling you knew Bowyer would fall to his knees like he'd just been shot to win the penalty.

The game was effectively over by the half-hour mark when Shearer tucked away the penalty to make it 3-1. We had our chances, with Keane hitting the bar and Jenas forgetting he had to roll the ball into an empty net rather than into the side of it after a glorious run. However, they were but small mirages of hope in a black and white striped desert. We were to be cast further adrift when Michael Dawson was rightly dismissed for his second bookable offence. We'll miss him badly for our next two games, unless Ledley comes back to set an example to big Tony. The latter always looks a slightly better bet with The King telling him what to do.

As if the loss wasn't bad enough, I have just witnessed the Goons getting through to the Champions League semi-finals at the expense of a truly rubbish side, supposedly called Juventus. What is it with the French Foreign Legion that every 'great' side they've come up against has performed like a bunch of rejects from The Three Stooges tribute act auditions? First it was Real Madrid and now the doddery Old Lady wheezed through 180 minutes of misplaced passes and attacking inability. One can only assume that the giant-killing Villarreal will now revert to their former mediocrity in time for their semi-final against the life-suckers.

I'm really starting to get worried about the whole losing out to the Goons scenario if we get fourth place because they've sneaked the Champions League. I know we still have to get that spot first but it would be just their style of stealing something eleven days after we rightly claimed it. Why the country who wins the competition isn't rewarded with an extra place is beyond me.

The fun starts again on Saturday with a lunch-time kick-off against Manchester City. It's a game we have to win and I'll be there, probably bleary-eyed at such an early Saturday time, cheering them on as if the Newcastle debacle never happened.

Saturday April 8th 2006

FA Premiership
Tottenham Hotspur 2 Manchester City 1
Attendance – 36,167
Spurs goalscorers – Stalteri, Carrick

Wednesday April 12th 2006

I THOUGHT I'D wait until the Arse made up their game in hand before making a judgement on this week's activities. I've just watched Harry Houdini's boys steal a point from the French at Fratton Park and suddenly everything seems a little rosier.

Three points from our game with Manchester City while the chasing Goons only picked up a solitary point from their two encounters. There's a four-point gap now between us and them, although that doesn't mean anything with our remaining fixtures, but it does provide a healthy cushion. What it also means is that if all results were to go our way over the Easter period then we may just assure ourselves of European football through the league for the first time since Pontius Pilate told a certain bearded fellow not to cross him.

It all began with an efficient performance against City which would have seen a more emphatic scoreline were it not for the wonder that is David James. The calamitous 'keeper is one of the best shot-stoppers around but he has the concentration levels of a four-year-old boy at a lecture on nuclear physics. When he tried to dribble the ball past Speedy Lennonalez with the delicacy of a pirouetting hippopotamus and presented Mido with the ball, I turned to the guy in the seat next to me and simply smiled. Today was going to be fun.

However, Mido did somehow contrive to miss the chance, which perhaps galvanised James, who sniggered his usual "Aren't I funny" grin to any team-mate who could bear to look at him. He then proceeded to save almost every shot that was fired at him, all bar the two which would prove crucial.

Robbie Keane was once again on another level. I've run out of superlatives to hurl at the skilful Irishman. He's easily playing the best football of his career mentally and physically. Despite his still tender years, he's one of the most experienced players at the club nowadays and thus his leadership qualities have skyrocketed. Obviously, taking on the Republic of Ireland captaincy has helped that build no end.

His team-mates, for once, weren't stumbling in his wake. Both full-backs had probably the best games of their Spurs careers. Paul Stalteri reacted excellently to being left out for the whining Stephen Kelly. Not only did he defend solidly, but even the defensive Yoda Alan Hansen pointed out how far he had run to convert the rebound from Keane's parried shot.

On the other side, Lee was excellent. He's got better and better as the season has progressed and his knowledge and understanding of the English game and language has improved. He learned the hard way that defenders in the Premiership are going to be hit and hit hard. It must be intimidating as a 3ft 4ins player to suddenly be faced with 90 minutes in the ring with Alan Shearer, Marlon Harewood et al.

However, the South Korean is learning to adjust by utilising his pace and reactions and is often nipping the ball away from cumbersome forwards and giving as good as he gets. Going forward, I'd say he's one of the best attacking full-backs in the Premiership. I was right about big Tony as well. Despite his dire display last week, the returning Ledley took him under his world-class wings and guided him through the game.

In the engine room, Jenas and Carrick proved once again that they are our best midfield pairing. Carrick's reluctance to step into the enemy's half, except to take corners and free kicks, gives Jenas licence to roam and attack at will. The young midfielder has the energy and pace to sprint all day from box to box. As for Carrick, I'm starting to think that he has access to my thoughts somehow or someone else with similar views has been slapping him in the face with videos of his set-pieces. I almost keeled over in surprise as he whipped in cross after free kick rather than dollying them up into the atmosphere.

In contrast to the performances of those on the pitch, I was more disappointed by the antics of the benched Edgar Davids. I've staunchly stuck by The Pitbull while others have said his influence and legs are fading with the advancing season. He was a substitute on Saturday for the first time for a long time and didn't he look delighted? I watched the highlights on my return on Football First and I doubt anyone missed him mouth "What's the point?" to Danny Murphy when he came on at the end of the game.

I understand you're frustrated, Edgar, but your replacement, Teemu Tainio, had a fine game, the manager's decision was justified, and we needed you to come on, waste some time and calm down the players in the final minutes. We all fought your corner when the media and other fans said you were going to upset team morale. We chose to ignore your incidents at other clubs. Please don't derail the train now when it's so close to the station.

The squad needs to take the confidence from the game into the Easter weekend's double header. I say squad rather than team because we have two games in three days against Everton at Goodison Park and Manchester United back at the Lane. It's going to be a difficult time and it'll be interesting to see whether Jol uses some of the fringe players who have been crying out for a game. The likes of Defoe, Murphy, Huddlestone, Kelly and Davenport must be in with a shout of getting some action.

It's a conundrum. Do you go with a slightly weaker side to take on a tough Everton side at their place or do you go all out and risk running out of steam against the Red Devils? We need our pacey, attacking players such as Lennon and Jenas to be flying when needed, not creaking and aching. What I do know is that if we can get a decent return from these games, then we carry on piling the pressure on that lot down the road. Then comes April 22nd.

Saturday April 15th 2006

FA Premiership
Everton 0 Tottenham Hotspur 1
Attendance – 39,856
Spurs goalscorer – Keane

Monday April 17th 2006

FA Premiership
Tottenham Hotspur 1 Manchester United 2
Attendance – 36,141
Spurs goalscorer – Jenas

WHAT AN EASTER weekend. On Saturday night I had singing bluebirds on my shoulder and was whistling 'Zip-a-dee-doo-dah'. Tonight, I feel like I've been punched in the gut by a ginger Scouse kid with the hopes of a country on his shoulders.

Against Everton, we were superb. As with the Man City game, had we converted more of our well-made chances we could have thrashed the Merseysiders. Keane and Defoe worked brilliantly and I'm starting to think that that partnership could be our best. Mido has looked out of form since the African Nations Cup and his injury will be a godsend to Defoe in his bid to make the World Cup squad.

Now we've got the players to control a game, the smaller forwards make us play some cracking football on the ground. Two small strikers fail when you are under pressure and have to boot the ball clear. However, we're now at the stage and have the players to ensure we don't find ourselves under the cosh. By all means have a big man on the bench in case that situation does arise. However, Defoe is getting sharper and sharper. He was instrumental in most of our attacking play today and he's so strong on the ball. The shot that hit the bar was Defoe at his best – making space for himself and dispatching an effortless shot past the 'keeper. Shame the bar went and spoiled it all. The bespectacled Swede watching in the stands must have been impressed, if he bothered to stay that long.

There were no duff performances throughout the side and Murphy got a good 45 minutes under his belt. Even David Moyes was gushing in his praise after the game. He said we were possibly the best side to have played at Goodison Park this season and said that they couldn't touch us, let alone create a decent chance. Even the introduction of Psycho Duncan couldn't unsettle the Spurs defence.

I can't help but laugh whenever the old Scot enters the fray. I always see Jimmy Bullard's face during the Wigan–Everton game, after Ferguson punched Paul Scharner in the stomach. Bullard tried to say something and just ended up laughing to his mates at this nutter who was still being thrown onto a football pitch.

Back to the Lilywhites. We were always in control, despite the referee playing five-and-a-half minutes of injury time instead of the three he'd told his assistant. It was a triumphant Saturday, but the Spurs rollercoaster took only two days to jolt suddenly and send me smashing into the hand-rail.

Today started pretty crappily anyway with the news that Ledley our King was out for the entire run-in – our captain, our most influential player gone with a stress fracture to that famous sodding metatarsal foot bone. Another victim of Big Dunc, but at least for him and England he should be fit for the World Cup. With Big Tony suffering from altitude sickness, the responsibility of shackling Wayne Rooney and Ruud van Nistelrooy fell to the returning Michael Dawson and Calum Davenport on his first start for Spurs.

Despite that it was a typical Tottenham against the big boys game. We create some great chances, fail to convert them and get punished. We've put in good performances against Chelsea, United, Liverpool and the Goons this season and we've come away with three points in all so far from the encounters. The way we started, with Lennon ripping Silvestre to shreds, it seemed as if it was going to be our day.

The first goal was typical of United as well. All the pressure was on their goal with Dawson and Defoe going close, but a lighting-quick breakaway meant we would spend the rest of the game playing catch-up. Sounds familiar, doesn't it? Yup, the away games against Chelsea and United started in exactly the same fashion.

Then came The Rocky Horror Pyo. Lee had three opportunities to clear the ball into the stratosphere, but decided it was better to allow his international team-mate Park Ji Sung every chance possible to tackle him. I've no doubt had King been there, Lee would have had his life threatened if he didn't lump the ball away. Instead, he let himself be tackled and then dived to the floor as if shot by an assassin in the crowd, while Rooney rolled the ball home.

Talking of the crowd, the atmosphere was superb today. Even at 2-0 down, we were all singing our hearts out trying to inspire the boys on that lush green surface. Almost all of us, that is. The fools that booed Lee after that second goal should have been thrown out of the ground. What a big help that was. Smash the player's confidence even more when he was obviously feeling like crap. Thank goodness for the real fans who cheered on his next touch. We're behind our team no matter what, willing them on.

We almost did it as well. When Jenas stabbed in the ball, only minutes into the second half, it was certainly game on. Defoe's work in the build-up to the corner should not be overlooked. He fought the whole game against Ferdinand and the shockingly lumbering oaf-like Vidic to work opportunities for the team. Had he put away some of his early chances, I'd be shouting his name from the rooftops right now.

As I'm dishing out praise in defeat, Davenport had a cracker of a debut alongside the equally superb Dawson. The latter started his Spurs career in a massive game against Liverpool. Now the former has followed it up with an impressive first start against top opposition. His performance may mean the end for Gardner as first choice back-up.

Lennon was impressive once again, although he tired as the game went on, as expected after two games in three days. Energiser Bunny Jenas, on the other hand, seemed to still be flying in the latter stages. On the left, The Pitbull was in and out of the game on his return. Sadly, he didn't give us anything that Teemu Tainio wouldn't have, had he been fit. Unless he comes up with a display of old against the Goons, I fear he may be on his way back to Holland in the summer. If he does go, though, it will be having taught a class of fresh-faced kids a lesson or two.

With us behind the team, we went so close over and over again, even if the chances did dry up towards the end. It was great to see Lee Barnard come on for his debut. He deserved his chance with his goal-scoring for the reserves and what a team to take on in your first game. He must have been buzzing. He did reasonably well and his persistence won us a few decent free kicks. How wonderful it would have been if the home-grown lad had smashed in the equaliser in the dying seconds.

It's all hypothetical though and I'm still feeling sick in my stomach about the result, especially after the way we played in spells today and the whole game against Everton. I sat wearing a scowl the whole tube ride home. Mothers ushered the children away, telling them "not to bother the man in a Spurs shirt who looks like a serial killer". I swear

I heard one woman say that as I repeatedly smacked my programme against my leg.

I'm about to sit down and watch Bolton against West Brom. If the relegation battlers can pull a result out of the bag, then we've made it through that European door. The Wanderers are the only ones who can catch us now below sixth place. A loss would leave them with four games left to bridge a 13-point gap, so we'd have made the Uefa Cup with three games to go which would be a tremendous achievement.

However, the race for the Champions League is not over yet by a long way, but now pretty much everything hinges on that match next Saturday. Here's to a nicely knackered Arsenal side, disillusioned and downcast after a 3-0 home drubbing by Villarreal at the Library. Whatever happens, it's going to be the game to end all games. Come on you Spurs… please.

Saturday April 22nd 2006

FA Premiership
Arsenal 1 Tottenham Hotspur 1
Attendance – 38,326
Spurs goalscorer – Keane

Sunday April 23rd 2006

IRONY IS SOMETIMES a very beautiful thing. How could anyone keep a straight face when Arsène Whinger, almost in tears, calls the Spurs bench liars because they claimed they didn't see something?

How many times have we heard the lithe Frenchman declare with squinty eyes that he didn't see one of his players lunge maniacally into the opposition? His catchphrase has become a national joke, but yesterday he had the temerity to accuse someone of doing the same sort of lying.

I waited until today to write about the game which brought us European football, because I wanted to see all the quotes from the managers and players and see which side the media came down on, in case I was alone in my view that there was little wrong with the now infamous incident.

I saw two Arsenal players clatter into each other while Carrick dribbled away from them. They both began to get up as the ref, Steve Bennett, checked they were all right, before he continued to run on himself, indicating to the other players to play on. Martin Jol wasn't looking at the incident. He'd seen Davids was about to stray offside and told Carrick to "play, play, play" before the Dutchman went too far.

Davids and Keane were up against three Arsenal defenders, who were playing on. Davids crossed to Keane who tapped it in – legitimate goal. The referee had no concerns as both players were rising from the floor.

The majority of the media, barring the Arsène poster-waving Oliver Holt, have sided with Spurs and pointed to the hypocrisy of Wenger. On *Match of the Day* they suggested the Frenchman had gone overboard in his criticism and I've just watched *Goals on Sunday* on Sky as they've dissected the incident from all angles and sided with Jol. The Portsmouth keeper Dean Kiely said there was no way a team would put the ball out in that situation as both players were getting up.

Probably one of the best things about the furore was that it gave us yet another iconic image of Martin Jol. Whenever I see Whinger in the future, I will always picture him trying to square up to Jol. The giant Dutchman stands there with his hands behind his back, amazed that this skinny guy is moaning in his face before unleashing a verbal volley back at him. At this point, Arsène slinked backwards quickly into his own technical area.

I saw this Jol quote today in one of the papers and it only added to the moment: "All I can say is that when Wenger squared up to me on the touchline, I had to hold myself back because he doesn't know how strong I am." Brilliant. There's no one else in the Premiership who is as open and honest to the media as him and it's so refreshing.

Wenger's frustration was probably more born from the fact that his French Foreign Legion were absolutely overwhelmed by a crowing Spurs side until he brought on the star of his one-man team. Carrick, Lennon and Keane were phenomenal and the Goons looked terrified any time the trio picked up the ball. The Library earned its name yesterday. The Arsenal fans watched in total dismay as they witnessed the gap closing between their side and our emerging youngsters. They even took to that wonderful fan idea of booing your own players. They should be thankful that the controversy of our goal gave them something to shout about.

The watching Sven must surely be considering taking Lennondinho to the World Cup as his wild card. In the biggest game of his career so far, the youngster looked like he was out for a kickabout in the park. He was laughing, enjoying himself and, as predicted by my good self, skinning Flamini at every opportunity. He turned 19 only last week, but I don't think any left-back in the Premiership can stop him now, let alone as he learns and reaches his peak.

I'm big enough to hold up my hands and say I got our right-wingers' prospects mixed up. I predicted at the season's birth that Wayne Routledge would be our star this year, while Aaron would learn his trade in our reserve side. I couldn't have been further from the truth. Routledge is plying his trade on loan for Portsmouth, mostly as a substitute. Lennon on the other hand has become something very special and has risen from bench warmer to impact sub, and then from sometime starter to being an expected name on the team sheet. I still believe Wayne has an important part to play in our future. Maybe he needs to train up his left foot and become the answer to our issues on that side of the pitch.

The great thing about Lennon is that he doesn't just have pace. He's very clever in his use of the ball and skilful with his flicks and turns. He's also worked on his final ball on the training ground and he now creates endless decent chances for the forwards rather than hitting the ball into the crowd or careering off a defender.

Alongside him yesterday, Carrick was immense. It was probably his best ever performance for Spurs and he almost did a Ricky. What a run past player after player, rounding Hasselhoff in goal before running out of room and hitting the side netting. He's been doing a number of these runs in recent matches, showing a turn of pace that people keep telling him he doesn't have. I point once again to the work of Ricardo Moniz in this skill work. It's very difficult to get the ball off Carrick nowadays with all his turns, which embarrassed endless lines of Goons yesterday. He's a big-game player and hopefully the bespectacled Swede recognised that from his lofty position.

Keane was once again everywhere. His Messiah celebration in front of the Spurs fans after the goal while chaos was erupting behind him provided another iconic image. I felt sorry for Davids, who had one of his best Pitbull performances this season, who received two harsh yellow cards, leaving us to fight out the last couple of minutes with ten men. His experience was vital as he made a number of important interceptions and clearances. It was good to hear on Friday from Jol that Davids has another year on his contract and he can't see him going anywhere. That's another year of education for our blossoming young side from the Dutch master.

We had to cling on in those final minutes, but apart from Henry's class finish after a blatant yet unpunished foul on Stalteri by the new Kanu, Adebayor, there weren't any worrying shots on target. Something else that seems strange is that Henry doesn't seem to have been criticised for running the length of the pitch to celebrate in front of the Spurs fans after he equalised. Gary Neville got fined heavily for running half the length of the pitch to do the same, yet the Frenchman seems to be exempt from such action. Fair play to the striker as he did admit that Stalteri was fouled before the goal and said that if Spurs said they didn't see the injuries, then he believed them. However, it's just a little odd that his inflammatory celebration wasn't punished by an organisation that will dish out a yellow card to a player who dares to take his shirt off in front of his fans after scoring. Oh the great nipple taboo.

The gap is definitely closing in North London, whatever the irritated Frenchman may say. Without his world-class captain, Arsenal are a decent top-six side, while Spurs have proved this season that we are top four material and can only get better. If Wenger manages to chain his captain to the new Sell Out Stadium then they will continue to rely on him for success. If they lose him, then Spurs will overtake them in the next couple of seasons. Whether he goes or not, North London is witnessing a rebirth of a sleeping giant.

Yesterday's point means that not only do we keep Arsenal at bay, but it also means that we have qualified for Europe through our league position for the first time since the Premiership was formed. Well done Jol and the lads for a fantastic achievement. It's definitely the proudest feeling I've had for my team after years of overpaid, ageing celebrity players going nowhere.

That's not to say I'm content with the achievement. As I'm sure Martin is telling the boys, Champions League football is in our hands. The work's not done yet and we still have two tough games against a Bolton side still trying to get into Europe and West Ham at Upton Park. Win those and Villarreal or Ronaldinho will do the business in the Champions League against those "fair" and Senderos-less Goons.

Saturday April 30th 2006

FA Premiership
Tottenham Hotspur 1 Bolton Wanderers 0
Attendance – 36,179
Spurs goalscorer – Lennon

SOME BIG BLOKES came to White Hart Lane and tried to bully us, but a tiny bloke squirmed through their legs and won the day. It was a massive goal from little Aaron in front of the watching England manager.

Thank goodness I am writing this down rather than having to talk about it, because my vocal cords have been torn to shreds. Today I shouted, screamed, barked, moaned, cheered and bellowed. Then, when it was all over, I slapped my hands raw, applauding the players around the pitch.

Even a train journey home spent staring into the sweat-soaked armpit of a ridiculously overweight man, barely wearing an impossibly tight Spurs shirt, could not detract from a massive result at White Hart Lane.

Ode to Jol

Martin Jol always asks the fans to be the twelfth man and raise the roof. Today was no different and I arrived full of voice and was even roaring like an idiot when the player's practice shots rippled the back of the net, much to my mate's embarrassment. My fellow bellowers and I were to be rewarded for our support.

What a send-off for the White Hart Lane faithful. Three points against a side which has battered Spurs in the league every single season and come away with the points. Not today. They still battled, bruised and left us all punch-drunk at half-time wondering how we weren't losing. I can only assume that Martin Jol spent the interval telling the players they should be more scared of his physical side than Bolton's, especially if they found themselves bullied out of fourth spot in their own playground.

As the majority of the crowd walked off to grab a burger or snack downstairs, my mate and I sat to check out the phone pictures he'd been taking throughout the game. With a host of action to feast our eyes on, imagine my discomfort when most of the shots seemed to be of players' backsides as they were placing the ball for corners and free kicks. Looking nonplussed and more than a little embarrassed, he blamed it all on the phone which was hastily tucked away, and we decided not to communicate for the rest of the fifteen minutes.

The second half wasn't the prettiest example of the Premiership, but it showed that we had the character to overcome the biggest of opponents, even without the leadership of Ledley King, Edgar Davids and Robbie Keane who departed the fray injured at half-time. We did have the help of a rather lenient referee who missed one dodgy incident where Michael Dawson won the ball having steamrollered through Stelios to get it. There was another shout for a handball against the future England defender, but he could hardly help it when the heading machine, Kevin Davies, was smacking back into him.

Lennon, however, was the difference. Just when you think your side has kept him quiet, he bursts into the play with that electric pace which must be so demoralising for tiring defenders. Ricardo Gardner is probably one of the fastest left-backs in the Premiership, but even he was second to everything that went near the jet-heeled Oompa Loompa. If only Willy Wonka could find us another for our left-hand side. Are you watching, Sven? Shaun Wright-Who?

Another youngster impressed in front of us today with 45 minutes of grit, determination and flashes of talent. With Keano out of the game, Martin Jol threw on the reserve goal machine, Lee Barnard, who'd made his debut only in the last home game against Manchester United. And you know what? The boy did good.

He threw himself at everything and won more headers than Keane and Defoe combined in the first half. The most important thing he did was unnerve the Bolton back line into making sloppy passes and hoofing the ball out of play. He also managed one sublime chest trap that was a throwback to the glue-slathered chest days of Fredi Kanoute. He was also inches away from making the game safe in the dying seconds when he just couldn't turn a long goal kick from Robbo into a shot on target. Fair play, lad, you were given a chance and you didn't get stage fright in the Premiership theatre. With Keane's injury, you may just get a first start next weekend.

A word must also go to big Tony in defence who possibly had his best ever game for Spurs, battling the aerial power of Davies and co. He didn't panic and he didn't hoof, he just played it pure and simple as a defunct, manufactured pop group once said.

Ode to Jol

At the other end of the pitch I felt sorry for Jermain Defoe. With Rooney's painful break yesterday and doubts over Michael Owen's fitness, this was a chance for Defoe to say to the watching Sven "I'm brilliant, me". Unfortunately, this was one of those games where a small striker was only going to get battered by two big central defenders. The one man who could have changed all that for Defoe was the normally pinpoint Danny Murphy. Unfortunately, the latter was rustier than a nail in the *Titanic*, spraying balls all over the stands.

The pictures said it all when Jermain was substituted for Andy Reid. As everyone stood and clapped, the bespectacled Swede sat in his seat with the face of a man whose only exciting gameplan has broken his metatarsal. Well done as well to the returning Andy Reid. The last I saw of him was a distant figure chasing an icecream van down Seven Sisters Road. However, today's Reid was a far leaner figure and was instrumental in battling to keep the ball in the final minutes. I feared the Irishman might be on his way out, but perhaps not.

It was great to cheer and show our appreciation to Jol as he walked round to all corners of the ground after the game, thumbs up and booting footballs into the crowd. The man is the first real legend we've had at the Lane in a long time. He's effectively grabbed a sleeping giant by the collar and shaken it until it awoke, blinking at a new dawn.

Daniel Levy should also be thanked for all his backing to the big man. In his programme notes today he wrote: "We shall look to the future and to continue to do the best for the club – your club. I hope you feel today that we have given you your Tottenham back – it was always our aim." You certainly have, Danny boy. We have Europe next season, gained through our league position, and although there's still a load of drama to go, we've already had the best season certainly in my memory.

I've just watched a Martin Jol interview where he reminded the interviewer that Everton were labelled a sensation last season for finishing fourth with 61 points. We've got 65, 13 more than last year, and there's still a game to go. Where does that put the Jolly Babies in the scheme of things?

The only irritation is that despite the progression, we're now facing a bizarre parallel situation to last year. At the end of the last campaign, we were faced with almost a month of waiting for the Uefa Fair Play draw. Clutching at straws, we prayed that someone would pluck our ball out of a bag and we'd sneak into the Uefa Cup through the nicey, nicey fair back door.

This year, we've secured our place in that competition next season. Instead, if we beat West Ham on Sunday, we face an entirely different excruciating ten-day wait for the Champions League final. If our hopes of qualification to the top tournament in the world rests on that game, we will be cheering on Barcelona as if they were wearing white and navy against the French Foreign Legion.

Chapter Eleven

May
Let's Twist Again

Sunday May 7th 2006

FA Premiership
West Ham United 2 Tottenham Hotspur 1
Attendance – 34,970
Spurs goalscorer – Defoe

I'M WRITING THIS little bit an hour-and-a-half before the West Ham game and I'm in a complete state of shock. My fingers are actually shaking as it has just been announced that our most important game in years is still to go ahead despite seven Spurs players going down with food poisoning today.

It's like a horrible nightmare or something out of Sky One's *Dream Team*. On the eve of our biggest match of the season, illness strikes. All sounds a little fishy to me. Apparently, according to Sky News, the police have been called in too. I wonder where they ate last night. Probably some place with a Gooner-supporting chef. Who is writing this stuff?

There's still no news about who the stricken players are. Who will come in? We do have a decent-sized squad, but not in certain positions. We're currently stuffed up front and in both full-back positions if any of those players are ill. We already had a hospital full of players out anyway with injuries. Will Clive Allen have to lead his reserve players out?

Let's Twist Again

I'm starting to feel sick myself now. Spurs tried to get the game called off or delayed for a few hours, but the Premier League came along and decided it still had to be played. So we could have the situation where any fit players are thrown together with little or no recent playing or training experience of each others' games. We could end up with a back line with no cohesion or even a team of reserves and youth players out there.

It's so scandalous, unfortunate and bizarre that I still can't believe it's true. It's like a massive twist at the end of a movie. I half expect someone on the *Soccer Saturday* panel to start debating who Keyser Soze is? Here's hoping the stage is set for someone unexpected to write his own ending to this strange script. Why oh why is supporting Tottenham Hotspur the most bizarre experience in the world?

Should a 26-year-old man be this close to tears over a game? Our Champions League dreams went down the toilet this afternoon, literally, as our sick, fatigued players strived to keep us in the battle.

Why with Spurs is there always something happening in the background? We can't just win or lose in dull, drab normal style. Today it was bloody food poisoning. What's that all about? The eve of your biggest game in years and it turns out ten players get poisoned. I don't think my heart can take much more of this emotion tugging.

In true movie style, it's too much of a coincidence surely? The police and environmental health officers are currently at the five-star London Marriott West India Quay Hotel checking out what happened to the players' food. Samples are being removed from the remnants of the lasagne and chicken and steak buffet put out the night before. There's even rumours of foul play by members of an international betting ring after a flurry of bets were placed on the match in Asia before the news of the poisoning broke.

It's just so bizarre. The G14-loving Premier League will postpone a game because the grass is too wet, days before Arsenal are due to play an important Champions League game. However, when a Tottenham Hotspur team is wiped out through poisoning before a game worth £35m then it's a "sorry, that just wouldn't be right".

There were rumours flying around that the players were throwing up in the tunnel before the game and during half-time. People are even claiming the chef has been arrested by the Metropolitan Police! What a bloody circus. I know I've said it so many times before, but only Tottenham Hotspur could attract this sort of sideshow to proceedings.

I feel like sinking to my knees on the front lawn screaming the word "sabotage" over and over again. Well, I would, but my neighbour is a Gooner and he'd only run out and kick me when I'm down. Where's Miss Marple when you need her? Was it the Wenger in the kitchen with the poison? Send her to the Library ruins where they're allegedly burying the evidence.

I love the fact that Richard Scudamore, the Premier League supremo, made his decision about the seriousness of the Spurs situation at... wait for it... Highbury. Probably with David Dein staring sternly at him from across the directors' box, he decided he couldn't be bothered to travel the five minutes' journey across to the hotel before swiftly denying any postponement. Maybe he was enjoying the party too much.

I don't know what difference it would make if foul play is discovered by the police. There wouldn't be any link to a club, apart from a fan being involved. All I know is that the game was massively affected. Every time there was a stoppage, the players were coming over and gulping down as much liquid as they could. There have been unconfirmed reports that Aaron Lennon and Teemu Tainio collapsed after the game and were taken to hospital.

I wonder if, behind the scenes, Daniel Levy is socking it to the Premier League. He doesn't seem like the "Oh well, bad luck boys" type. Jol said after the game that if Spurs chose not to play the match, then they would have faced a Middlesbrough-style points deduction. However, I still worry that the decision to play will allow the FA to brush this under their red carpet.

I can barely bring myself to write about the game itself – I'm that distraught – but I'll try my best. Apparently, Carrick and Dawson were the worst hit by the poisoning and it showed. The team's spine was crippled and West Ham knew it. For the first 20 minutes, they spanked us left, right and centre. I have no idea how our young central defender was heading away balls despite bearing the grimace of a man who desperately needed to rush to the nearest loo.

Carrick got worse and worse as the game went on. All those toilet breaks throughout the day must have wiped out his body's hydration. Edgar Davids, who was superb today, screamed at the Spurs bench when they tried to take him off over Carrick, who was practically wheezing on his knees. As the Geordie went off, it was clear to see he said: "I'm f***ed". Fair play to Edgar. It seemed like a tantrum at the time, but he was rightly upset that they hadn't noticed Carrick and he wanted the best for the team. He was like an unleashed lion today and he won so many tackles, driving the team forward.

However, time and time again the players just couldn't get up to support the attacking play. The only player who looked sharp was Jermain Defoe. I'm not sure whether Sven was in the crowd, but at least Jermain got his groove back. His equaliser was classic Defoe, holding off the defender, a stylish turn and a sweet finish into the far corner.

I'm assuming Keano and Lennon were both among the poisoned players, as they were rarely there to help out their fellow attacker. The little winger hardly got out of first gear. For once the runs associated with Lennon weren't those on the pitch.

The sick players were definitely amazing in the way they heroically battled through adversity and there were times when I thought it was still going to be our day. Wet Spam missed so many chances and even Teddy Teddy contrived to miss a penalty. For a while the draws at both grounds meant we would finish in fourth place. Unfortunately, the majority of Spurs fans knew we couldn't rely on Reto and his Wigan team-mates to spoil the Library's last day and so it would be.

We were so close to the promised land of the Champions League. Instead we will battle it out in the Uefa Cup next year. Sure it's Europe and it's still been the best season in my Spurs memory, but I can't help but feel like throwing up alongside those brave Lilywhites. We've been fourth since December and we lose it on the last day to that lot. What a kick in the teeth.

All those last-minute goals hurt even more now. As great a campaign as it has been, we've shot ourselves in the foot so many times that fate was bound to force us to stumble over the line, behind the Goons. I've just read those last few lines back. You can tell when I'm writing far too soon after a game, because I turn into a moaning old git.

I'm whinging, yet my side have just finished the season in fifth place, 13 points and four places above last year's position, and have qualified for Europe through the league for the first time since the Premiership began. If someone had offered me fifth place last July I would have bitten off their hand before scoffing down the rest of their body in my greedy frenzy.

I can't turn over to Sky Sports News, because I'm scared of seeing fireworks and celebrations above the Library. Maybe as fans our thoughts were too settled on that Champions League final and buying our Barcelona shirts. Now that evening in Paris means nothing to our club, merely an opportunity to see Arsenal getting spanked by Ronaldinho and co.

I'm off to hide in a cupboard for a few days, wrapped in my Spurs towel, while I contemplate the meaning of life. I will hopefully come back refreshed and doused with perspective. Then I'll be able to reflect on the season as a whole, rather than a day of infamy.

Monday May 8th 2006

HAVE I FALLEN through some bizarre wormhole into another dimension where absolutely anything goes in football?

First we have mass food poisoning and now Sven Goran Eriksson watches some Arsenal kid training, a boy who has never played in the Premiership, and decides to take the child to the World Cup possibly.

Like Sunday, today's squad announcement was like being punched and kissed in equal measures. The news filtered through and first up was good old Robbo, England's Number One and then they went through the defence. Hang on a minute, where's Ledley? Then the midfield – Carrick, Jenas, Owen Hargreaves?... and, yay, Aaron Lennon. Now for the formality of the strikers and Jermain... bloody Theo Walcott???

Ode to Jol

After a weekend of Spurs fans screaming about Arsenal's influence within the FA's corridors of power, we have the most bizarre selection in the history of English football. After months of telling his players they must be playing regularly for their clubs, the nutty Swede goes and decides on the morning of the squad announcement that he is going to pick a 17-year-old who has never appeared for his club.

I do not doubt that Theo Walcott has the potential to be something special one day. However, at this point in time he has never been tested against a Premiership defence, let alone a world class-back line. Unless I'm much mistaken, I don't think he's even played more than a handful of reserve games for the Goons.

My son has never played in the Premiership and can't break into a top flight side, but Sven never comes to watch him kick the ball around in the garden. Maybe it's because I'm not a skinny French guy with selective vision. In the past, I have doubted the conspiracy theories about Arsenal influence through Wenger and David Dein. However, if they can convince the England manager that a kid they don't think is good enough to play for Arsenal at the moment is good enough for the national side, then who knows what they can pull off.

"Zis kid is de dog's nuts, Monsieur Eriksson," Wenger reportedly whispered to the Swede as they dined in the Arsenal canteen. If so, Whinger, then why has he not been ushered onto the pitch for even a minute during any of the 25 games that have taken place in a variety of competitions since he joined? Is Arsène saying that his Arsenal side are better than England? So if Adebayor was English he'd be in ahead of Walcott? I'm shuddering with the thought right now.

I feel so sorry for Jermain Defoe and the Premiership's top English goalscorer Darren Bent. Sven has almost ruined the former's game by dragging him back from his goal-poaching positions to become "more involved in the play". I notice he's never said that to Michael Owen. Yet after all the work the internationally experienced Defoe has put in and the goals Bent has scored, the Swede decides one morning on a whim to pick some kid who hasn't proven anything.

Effort and achievement obviously mean nothing to the bespectacled one. When asked how he made the decision to leave both out of the squad, he bizarrely admitted: "Probably not too logically." Who else wants to tear out their hair and gnash their teeth? At least Defoe is on a standby list of five and will probably replace Rooney if it's confirmed that the Manchester United striker won't make the finals. Knowing Sven though, even if there's a chance that Wayne could hobble around for a minute of injury time at the end of the final in July, that'll secure his place.

With only four strikers named, what could we end up with in the early games if we gamble on Rooney's fitness? What if Rooney and Owen are not ready and Crouch picks up a knock as the lone striker in the first game? We could have little, inexperienced Walcott struggling to jump half of the way up to long balls fired up the pitch, while bulky defenders walk all over him. The goalscoring records of Crouch and Theo hardly inspire confidence.

Thank goodness for Lennon. His inclusion is the one exciting piece of news to have come from the squad naming. This boy finally gives England a Plan B. When the side is looking jaded against a tactically excellent side, then Lennonaldinho can come on and change the game in an instant with his road runner legs. Even Paolo Maldini would crap himself at the sight of little Aaron tearing towards him with the ball.

I expect Carrick and Robbo to be involved during the tournament and it's a good experience for Jenas to go along and he may get some minutes on the pitch. The player I feel for, who has no chance of going to Germany, is Ledley King. Despite the fact that he is returning to light training and has had a month more to recover from the same injury as Rooney, Ledley is out.

Despite his flexibility and experience of major international games, Sven just couldn't wait for one of Europe's top defenders to get fit. Instead he calls up Owen "Have you ever seen me play?" Hargreaves, who has had a forgettable season hidden in the Bayern Munich squad, and the oh-so-reliable Campbell. How has Judas earned a role in the biggest tournament in the world over a recovering King or even a fully fit and more talented Michael Dawson? One rule for Sven's favourites, one for everyone else.

The only bonus for the King of the Lane is that in his press conference Sven did admit that if there is a problem with a central defender before the tournament, then he will look at Ledley's fitness and may call him in as a last-minute replacement. Not that I'd ever wish an injury on a player, Sol, but good luck Ledley.

It's been a weird day, but I'll still cheer on England and my crowing lions, with more than a little fear mixed in with the World Cup excitement. If we can still win the thing, it'll be despite the best efforts of an easily led Swede.

Tuesday May 16th 2006

LOOKING TO NEXT season and we've signed a massive £34m four-year shirt sponsorship deal with the gaming company Mansion. Apparently, it's one of the ten biggest sponsorship deals in the world. If that's not a massive stride forward for the club, then I don't know what is.

According to the club, Mansion will "help Tottenham promote its brand in Asia and other international markets, develop an international supporters' club and set up a co-branded internet gaming site." The company is controlled by billionaire Putera Sampoerna, Indonesia's third-richest man. More power to the table for Tottenham Hotspur. When I close my eyes, I can see a Lilywhite army marching across Asia, gathering supporters at every turn.

Well done to Daniel Levy and the businessmen behind the scenes for that spot of deal making. They nipped in after Manchester United mucked around in their dealing with Mansion, and negotiations fell apart.

With the deal, the new shirt was released. It will appeal to those who wanted the navy arms ripped off the shirt as the front is back to the classic Spurs all-white look, barring a small navy trim on the sleeves. The back is a slightly different story with a blue arc, but that looks rather cool. It is on the whole suitably classy, although for some reason I keep thinking Derby County when I see the front. The Mansion logo also means we have another splash of red on our tops, but for £34m I guess we can make some concessions and at least it's not a big red smile grinning at us.

A small portion of that £34m sponsorship money is heading into our football in the community project which can only increase our fan base and talent pool across London and the surrounding counties. The rest of the bounty will hopefully go on squad building and stadium improvement.

Regarding squad building, the transfer window has only just opened, but that hasn't stopped half of the football world being linked with Tottenham Hotspur. Players from Brazil to Timbuktu are all apparently "set to sign" in the next 48 hours. If certain reports are to be believed then Ronaldinho and Zico will soon be paraded in the new Puma kit on the hallowed turf.

The silly season has begun, when 'insiders' and 'sources close to' crawl out like ants from every available nook and cranny to comment on club affairs. In the past, the word Tottenham was used by agents across the world to increase interest in their clients or snare better deals at their current clubs. If in doubt see Rivaldo, Edgar Davids or Mark Van Bommel's books on the subject, available in all disreputable bookstores.

That was then; now a buzz surrounds White Hart Lane. If Damien wants them, they will come. All he probably needs is to quote Daniel Levy's brilliant line: "In a world of Uniteds, Citys and Rovers, there is only one Hotspur." What fool wouldn't sit open-mouthed before signing on the dotted line?

According to both Bayer Leverkusen and Wigan Athletic we have bid for Dimitar Berbatov and Pascal Chimbonda and met the release clause for the former. I'd be delighted with both those signings. The Bulgarian Berbatov is a natural goalscorer with power, height and pace. The 25-year-old has notched more than 20 goals in each of the past few seasons and boasts a terrific record at international level. Critics will no doubt wave Sergei Rebrov posters at us when they find out we're believed to be splashing out £10.7m on the hitman.

Berbatov is no Rebrov though. He's big and strong and the German league is probably the closest league physically to the Premiership. If the rumours are true, we beat off the Goons and Manchester United to complete a deal. I read in the German press that after Berbatov's last game for Leverkusen, in which he scored his 21st league goal of the season, he thanked the club and then said: "I have a new task now at Tottenham Hotspur, which I will tackle." That sounds pretty definitive and like a man on a mission. Your number nine shirt is waiting on the peg for you, Dimitar.

I'm guessing his arrival means we won't be making Mido's loan move permanent. Had he kept up his pre-African Nations form then I may have been more disappointed, but he's dropped off considerably since his exploits in Egypt. Berbatov seems to be more of a natural goalscorer with a higher work ethic, but with a similar physique to the Egyptian. Keane and Defoe have proved they can play together again and with the Bulgarian will make a lethal trio.

As for Chimbonda, Wigan have rejected £2m and £3m bids from us for the pacey right-back. We don't usually give up when we have someone in our sights – see the year-long chases of Andy Reid and Wayne Routledge for examples of that – so we'll probably snare him eventually. Hopefully, he'll make more of an instant impact than that duo though. He was named in the Premiership team of the season and he has certainly been integral to Wigan's success, even if giving his transfer request on the pitch wasn't the classiest thing to do. Did he have it in his sock?

He was a shock call-up for France for the World Cup despite never being called up under Raymond Domenech before. That'll add another couple of million to the transfer fee. The French coach has done a Lennon – calling up a class player who has form and momentum in his favour. That's as opposed to a Walcott – where you call up a kid you've never seen play, and pray the opposition will be scared of the unknown rather than laughing at you.

Chimbonda looks like the next step up on Paul Stalteri, who in turn was an upgrade on Stephen Kelly, despite some last-minute horror shows. As Jol said last month,

Kelly has his heart set on leaving, so farewell kid. Don't let the White Hart Lane door smack you on the backside as you leave and remember what happened to our last departing right-back called Stephen. Who? Exactly.

Ah, the silly season at White Hart Lane. I adore it. I truly am a total THFC addict. Maybe I am a sad nerd, but I get a chill up my spine whenever I turn on the radio, computer or television or spy a newspaper back page in a shop and spot that eye-catching headline about my club. Just the merest chance that such a Galactico could come to the white side of North London is enough to make the heart skip a beat. Don't bother me with quotes or facts, I need to dribble and dream for a few days.

To top it all off this year, we have a World Cup to look forward to with one of the strongest Tottenham contingents in decades, if not the strongest ever. I'll be proudly cheering on our lads and hope that glory beckons for them and the country. Hopefully, it will be a month-long festival of football with a Lilywhite core which will see football finally coming home.

Tuesday May 30th 2006

I'M CONVINCED THAT Sven Goran Eriksson is either completely mad or a Dr Evil-style megalomaniac who puts his little finger to the corner of his mouth in quiet moments and emits an evil laugh.

What other reason could there be for him deciding on a whim to throw Jamie Carragher into the holding role that has Michael Carrick glowing in neon lights above it? I'm guessing he chickened out of his original choice of David James for the part as his diabolical plot may just have been uncovered then.

I don't understand how he can justify putting the central defender into the position in tonight's friendly against Hungary ahead of the most in-form English player in that role. Not only that but he decides that without having seen Carragher in the holding role in an international that the line-up is his one for the World Cup. What is his deal with deciding things without ever seeing them in the flesh?

The result was probably the most boring England game I've witnessed in years. I may have lapsed into a coma were it not for Peter Crouch and his shocking robot dancing. Thank the lord for your crazy moves, Peter. For 40 minutes in the first half especially, Sven's 'brilliant' new formation utilising the attacking talents of Steven Gerrard and Frank Lampard managed to make world-class players look like confused, ponderous 16-year-olds plucked from a reserve side.

There were no Hungarian attacks for the defensive Carragher to break up, so the guy – who is an excellent central defender – could only showcase his sideways and backwards passing. The game was crying out for Carrick to release all those attacking players with his pinpoint sprayed passes across the pitch.

I'm getting worried about Michael Owen. He doesn't look a player who is trying to get fitness back before a major tournament. A player of his calibre would still be getting touches of the ball and hitting slightly wayward shots. Owen is not even getting near the ball or the surrounding action. His header before the dubious penalty was the only time I remember him touching the ball. I hope the rumours aren't true about his foot not being properly healed and him being rushed into action because of the Rooney circus.

The only players who shone in the game tonight were David Beckham and Peter Crouch. The former's crossing and set-pieces were further proof that this aspect of his game is unsurpassed in world football at the moment. The latter followed up a decent performance for the England B side against Belarus last week with an excellent substitute appearance tonight. His flicks and possession play were superb and his goal was clinical. I wasn't too keen on him to begin with, but I'm warming to the BFG and I'm no longer terrified about him entering the field of play.

It was nice to see that Sven rewarded Aaron Lennon for his man of the match performance for the England B side with his first international cap. Oh no wait, he didn't. I think the Swede likes the idea of picking Spurs players in his squad, but doesn't want them to dislodge any of his 'boys'. It took a number of high profile mistakes and constant media pressure before he allowed Robbo to replace Calamity James in goal. Similar national feelings are building about Carrick getting in the side and Defoe being added to the side. Will he cave in in time to save England's chances?

How much longer can he let Owen Hargreaves prove his ineffectiveness at international level? Yes, Sven, I agree that most of us haven't seen the young man in action in the Bundesliga this season. However, it doesn't take a German football aficionado to notice that in his last two games, Hargreaves has given the ball away 942 times and made 3,346 fouls.

Ya, for sure he is versatile and is cover for the worst of situations in a few positions, but Carrick must have been punching the walls of the Old Trafford dugout as he watched the Canadian/German/Englishman fudge pass after pass.

Will Sven also continue to throw Theo Walcott into action like a small wide-eyed lamb to the slaughter? The kid obviously has decent technique and the potential to be a very good player, but it's hardly like chucking the similarly aged Wayne Rooney into the fray. Rooney was and still is built like Mike Tyson, whereas Walcott is built like the kid out of *Different Strokes*.

Some corners of the media are trying to get people excited about him, but he's just not with the pace in games. I thought Sven was doing a USA 94 Ronaldo thing with the kid, taking him for the experience rather than game time, but worryingly that doesn't seem to be the case. I hope for the nation that Theo proves me wrong, but I just can't see how he is a better option than a fresh yet experienced Jermain Defoe.

With regards to Spurs on the home front in the last week or so, the Berbatov deal has been sealed which is excellent news. We splashed out an almost club record £10.9m on the Bulgarian hitman. I wonder if that figure was deliberately just short of Sergei Rebrov's £11m fee to avoid comparisons. Judging by the physical differences between the two, I don't think the comparison will end up being fair.

Berbatov said all the right things on making the move. Not only did he say he was going to fire us into the Champions League next season, but he brought a smile to all Lilywhites by revealing that he snubbed a move to Manchester United to join the "excellent" Martin Jol and his side which are going places.

The Chimbonda deal has still not happened and I'm undecided about it. I still think he's a step up on Stalteri, but he comments that he would love to go to Manchester United, but only Tottenham have bid for him. Fair enough, he still admits he would like to come to Spurs and I'm sure most footballers would love to play for Man Utd, but you just don't say it when you are close to a deal with Spurs. It's not exactly dispelling his mercenary image.

There's been plenty of links with other players. The majority of betting seems to be on Carlton Cole joining as a fourth striker. As a fourth striker he's a good buy, who could learn and develop from the others ahead of him. If, however, he ends up being a cheap replacement for Jermain Defoe, then I may just jump from the top of the cockerel on the stadium roof. If we sell that kid, then he will score 20 plus where he goes – might as well dispose of Robbo, King and Carrick while we're at it.

I almost had a heart attack when I saw a headline last week that read 'Spurs sign Sven'. Fortunately, it was an 18-year-old starlet named Sven Verdonck from Belgian side Genk. The story has since been denied by the kid's club, but stories surrounding previously unknown youngsters normally turn out to be true.

We've also been linked with the Brazilian Denilson and Damien Duff. The former fills me with a reasonable amount of excitement as long as he's a team player, but the latter would be the icing on the cake. In my mind Duff is the best left-winger in the Premiership. If Robbie Keane could sway him with a Guinness then it would be our biggest signing in a while. Just imagine him and little Aaron attacking from both sides. I bet Kolo would have an accident just thinking about it.

With all the incomings there have been some outgoings – all of which I'm not too bothered about. Farewell Noureddine Naybet and Goran Bunjevcevic. Both of you were excellent servants to the club and, from what I've heard, helped the youngsters on no end. Ledley King learned so much from Naybet while the reserves benefited from Bunje's experience. Both players played with passion for the club and that won't be forgotten.

Mido has also walked like an Egyptian all the way back to Roma after being told his loan deal would not be made permanent. Had he finished the season in the way he started it then I'd be a little distressed. However, he was plagued by injury and didn't look anywhere near as trim as he did in the early season.

There were also unconfirmed reports of differences with Martin Jol and that Roma wanted far too much for him. His replacement would seem to be the prolific Berbatov, who is also good in the air but scores far more goals on the deck. Good luck to Mido though, as well as Naybet and Bunje. They all did their bit over the last couple of seasons.

Who knows what could happen on Saturday in England's final friendly against Jamaica? What worries me is that it should be a cricket score even if we put out eleven Owen Hargreaves. Oh god, I shouldn't have said that... wait... who's that bespectacled balding bloke running away scribbling into a notepad?

Chapter Twelve

June
Lilywhites on the World Stage

Sunday June 4th 2006

WHAT A STRANGE couple of days it has been. Owen Hargreaves didn't even get on the pitch for England, Arsenal are being investigated over dodgy dealings in Belgium with the threat of Champions League expulsion, David Dein got told to sling his hook from the FA board and Peter Crouch scored a hat-trick.

It all started with the news that BBC's *Newsnight* programme had discovered evidence that the Belgian outfit Beveren had received an anonymous £1m investment, which the authorities traced back to the good old Goons. It was also reported that Beveren chairman Franz Van Hoof – what a cracking name – told police that Arsène's lads were the main shareholders of NV Goal – a company which effectively controls the club.

Although nothing illegal took place, FIFA's lawyers are investigating whether Emirates FC have broken their rule which forbids any club to control another in any way whatsoever. If the Goons, who vehemently deny any wrongdoing, are found to have breached this rule, they could be heavily fined or even suspended from the Champions League. I guess the next English club would have to take their place. I wonder who they are?

When I heard that FIFA would take action based on a report from the FA, I began to hear the sound of things being swept under a carpet. Then I switched on Sky Sports News to hear that David Dein's re-election to the FA board had not gone as swimmingly as he had expected. The chairmen of the other clubs had decided that they'd prefer someone else in his place. Some have suggested that the breaking of the Beveren story seemed almost too perfectly timed.

I guess when you annoy the likes of Steve Gibson at Middlesbrough, Big Sam and his mate Phil at Bolton and Super Danny down the road, they'll only start tugging at loose threads on your smartly pressed FA-badged jacket.

While that was raging on and Spurs fans chortled into their Champions League final programmes, there was the small matter of the last England game before the World Cup against Jamaica. Ex-Spur Peter Crouch helped himself to two-and-a-half goals, and a truly shocking penalty miss.

It was hardly a game of note as the commentators' curse struck again. As soon as the words "this is much more of a test than England's final warm-up game against Iceland before Euro 2004" stumbled out, Jamaica were buried under an avalanche of shots and goals and it ended up 6-0, better than the Iceland score.

From the Spurs contingent, Robbo had very little to do in goal apart from beat away one long-range shot. Carrick and Lennon came on later in the game when England were already 5-0 up and there was nothing left to show.

Lennon looked oddly reluctant to run at people, often passing the ball back to Carragher behind him. Carrick looked more assured and provided the pass of the match to Lennon which led to Crouch's shockingly misjudged attempt at a penalty.

Jermain Defoe is going with the squad to Germany.

Ode to Jol

Whether he stays there for two days or a month or so is dependent on the results of Wayne Rooney's scan on Wednesday. It's got to the point where the Rooney saga just needs to be sorted one way or the other. The Scouse wonder is without doubt the best player in England and if there is a definite chance he will be fully fit for the knockout stages of the competition then, fine, take the lad.

However, if there is only a slim chance he will play some part in the finals, then he shouldn't go. Not only will a rushed-into-action Rooney not be fair on himself or the viewing public, if something goes wrong with his foot then the career of an amazing 20-year-old with four or more World Cups ahead of him could be finished. Is it worth losing such a talent over a month's football?

Jermain Defoe can do the business for his country if called upon. I'd love a fully fit Rooney to tear apart the world's best sides, but little Jermain is a very capable replacement. I can just see him replicating his Arsenal goal last year against Brazil in the final. Wow, what a thought.

The World Cup is under a week away now and the excitement levels are starting to grow. The terrible unofficial England anthems on the radio are getting stuck in my head and even the tacky St George car flags are making me think of sitting with a cold beer, a steak cooking on the barbecue and our first game against Paraguay on the television. Roll on the Samba beat, the Italian moans and the English roar.

Saturday June 10th 2006

World Cup Group B
England 1 Paraguay 0
Attendance – 48,000
England goalscorer – Paraguay's Carlos Gamarra

IT ALL STARTED so well and then Sven got his hands on the game. With a couple of baffling substitutions he helped dry up the ideas for an England team battling the heat.

How come England always struggle with the heat in World Cups? They know the tournament is always going to be played in the summer sun, yet we always hear after games that the "South Americans adapted to the heat better". Why don't the English players spend a month in Dubai before the finals adapting themselves?

Just when I thought the spectre of Owen Hargreaves had departed to the shadows of the dugout, Sven flung him into the breach in a Superman costume, which promptly melted in the Frankfurt furnace. To show that the England set-up has grown and developed since Euro 2004, the Swede dealt his ace card by once again, à la Portugal, deciding that the skill on the bench was not enough, he needed his little Owen. I think the Canadian/German touched the ball once.

I told everyone I knew that despite my reservations about Michael Owen's fitness, he would come good in the World Cup, because he's a big-game player. I reserve the right to that opinion because although I saw his name on the team sheet, the England vice-captain didn't actually turn up for the first game of the tournament. Peter Crouch was knocking down headers into the space where he should have been all afternoon.

With my Spurs hat on, Paul Robinson didn't have a

lot to do bar scaring the crap out of a Paraguay player by running at him with his hands outstretched while he attempted a shot.

Even England fans with no club allegiances would have suggested Aaron Lennon and Michael Carrick were far more logical choices than Downing and Hargreaves as substitutes. Lennon would have brought pace to the table to terrify the Paraguayans and Carrick would have held the ball and used it far better than our curly-haired friend.

The Lilywhite who was missed the most, though, was the little guy who was sitting with his feet up at home watching the game on his television, probably spitting at the screen every time the bespectacled Swede appeared. The game was crying out for Jermain Defoe to come on for Michael Owen. The whole world knows now that Sven realises he has committed the biggest cock-up of his reign.

Maybe someone has sat down with the balding manager – hopefully Steve McClaren for the sake of England's future – and explained that it would have been just about acceptable to take a 17-year-old who hasn't even played a Premiership game, if there were three fit strikers ahead of him.

However, Sven has taken Theo Wal'cot't when he has only one fully fit forward in Peter Crouch. The time for experiments and 'exciting' gambles is not now. From the quotes coming from David Beckham, Steven Gerrard and the Swede himself, Defoe has knuckled down in training and impressed everyone and put Theo in the shade. Has any player said anything about the child in the last few weeks?

The problem for Sven was that until yesterday Jermain could only have come into the squad at Rooney's expense, which was never going to happen. Everyone's been talking about Defoe's goals and work rate in training – Beckham even called him "one of the best players in Europe". I'm guessing Theo has followed his rabbit-in-the-headlights friendly performances with similar fish-out-of-water training sessions.

By putting Downing on today and pushing Joe Cole into the second striker role, Sven admitted that he's made a monumental mistake and Walcott is not ready for the big time yet. Even as the game went on and England needed an outlet up front, the only striker on the bench was not turned to. As I've said before, I hope for England's sake the boy comes good, but it's yet another kick in the teeth for Defoe.

I just hope the diminutive poacher doesn't take his frustrations out on Tottenham. His exclusion was nothing to do with his substitute appearance in Spurs' second half of the season. He still appeared more than 30 times for the club last season and after Mido went missing in a pie shop, he started almost every game. Hopefully someone will point out to him that even when he was playing every game and scoring freely, Sven still left him out of his line-up against Wales for no apparent reason.

It was good to see Martin Jol come out and blast Sven for his bizarre selection policy that involved talking to Arsène Wenger and calling up one of his reserve youngsters to the biggest stage in the world. With talk of a £12m bid from Portsmouth and Liverpool needing a striker, I hope Defoe realises that all he needs is a break as Keane did and his Spurs career could explode into action on the European trail.

Talking of rumoured bids, there has been a lot of confirmed transfer activity around White Hart Lane in the last few days. The biggest probably has been Manchester United's £10m bid for Michael Carrick.

Only a Scotsman could try and mess with the head of an England player on the eve of the World Cup. Jol has come out since and said we sent them packing as Carrick is not for sale.

Other news sources have said that we told the Red Devils to stump up double that and maybe we'll talk. £20m may be enough to wipe my tears away as with that money you could buy most players in the world, but Carrick has become Tottenham Hotspur. I called him the Ghost of White Hart Lane last season, but he has matured into one of the best holding midfielders in the world. Who could we find that's better? We have Tom Huddlestone coming through, but he won't be at Carrick's level for a season or two.

The coming weeks will show how badly Sir Alex wants to replace Roy Keane. There are rumours that Carrick was offered a similar contract to Ledley King and turned it down, saying he will see out his four years and then go. As always, that kind of information comes from fans who know a man who owns a dog which peed on Daniel Levy's car once. Sometimes it's true, but most of the time it's complete rubbish. I'm hoping in this case it's the latter and Carrick signs a new deal and puts an end to the speculation.

Damien Comolli has brought in two new young talented faces in Benoit Assou-Ekotto from Lens and Dorian Dervette from Lille. The former is considered to be the best left-back in France. At 22, the French/Cameroonian has European experience and can play at left-back, left central midfield and left wing. Reports stated that we battled it out with the Goons for his signature. He sounds like a starter rather than a squad member, so that either means Lee is being switched to right-back or one of the two will push up onto the left wing.

Dorian Dervette is an exciting buy and is probably one to come through over the course of the next couple of seasons. He's the France U18 captain, is 6ft 4ins and apparently has tremendous technical skill according to our Sporting Director. A little birdie also told me that he turned down Chelski to come to us. Unlucky, Frankie Boy.

There have been a few departures with Stephen Kelly finally getting his wish to play for a lesser club. The club cunningly took up an option to extend his contract by a year so they could demand a fee from Birmingham for the wantaway Irishman. He has the potential to be a decent player in that league, so good luck to him. I'll always remember his cracking goal in the 5-1 demolition of Aston Villa last year.

The other departure is a sadder one for me. Mounir El-Hamdaoui has returned home to Willem II in Holland. Reports were that he was very homesick and he was so unlucky with injuries. Every time he got close to the squad or had a decent spell on loan at Derby, he picked up another serious knock. I hoped he was one for the future, but the arrival of Berbatov meant that he was going to stay down the pecking order. As with Kelly, I will remember him for a single moment: a wonderful piece of skill during last summer's Peace Cup when he turned into Ronaldinho for a moment and wowed all Lilywhites.

The World Cup football feast continues this week after a decent start and some great goals. Thursday brings with it Trinidad and Tobago after their heroic ten-man goalless draw against Sweden. The bosses at work are actually allowing us drones to leave the building early to get back for the 5pm kick-off. My mate has bet me that Jermaine Jenas doesn't get one minute of playing time in the tournament. I wonder if I've got enough time to get to Germany and threaten a Swede.

Thursday June 15th 2006

World Cup Group B
England 2 Trinidad and Tobago 0
Attendance – 41,000
England goalscorers – Crouch, Gerrard

Sunday June 18th 2006

IN THE SPACE of a week I've been impressed with two players past and present who have lit up the World Cup stage.

During the week I enjoyed one of those rare moments when working at a local newspaper throws up something that I really enjoy, such as the Spurs friendly earlier in the season. This time my assignment was to interview former Spur, World Cup winner and World Cup Final goalscorer Martin Peters after a signing session for his new book *The Ghosts of 66*.

To say I was slightly nervous was an understatement, almost to the point of passing off the chance to someone else. Then I slapped myself sharply. The man is a legend. Not only had he won a suitcase full of trophies at White Hart Lane, but he's held aloft the prize that David Beckham serenades in his sleep. For the next half an hour, I wrote down as many questions as I could possibly squeeze into my allotted five minutes' interviewing time, obviously crow-barring Spurs into every nook and cranny.

I walked down to the Ottakar's bookstore where the session was taking place. There wasn't much chance of missing it. The queue was spilling out of the shop and down the High Street. The lunchtime heat beat down on the sweaty heads of football fans young and old. Some were there to buy a book for Father's Day and get the great man to slap his mark on it. Then there were the eBay types with their suitcases full of photos and posters for him to sign.

I made myself known to his polite public relations assistant, whose name went in one ear and plopped onto the floor behind me. Then I stood in a corner, watched the excitement and waited for the enormous queue to clear so I could get my chance to chat with a World Cup winner. I've taken my son to Spurs signings at the club shop before, but Martin showed how the pros do it.

Unlike the young stars of today who are allowed to give their adoring young fans a quick autograph and if lucky a half-smile for the cameras, the ex-Spur spoke to every person as if they were a friend. Even when the eBayers got to his table, he was polite and agreed to sign a few things but nothing excessive. What surprised me most was the number of people in the queue who were related to ex-team-mates of his. He was constantly saying things like "of course I remember old Johnny boy" and then eulogising about them.

All this time spent with the fans meant that I stood for over an hour propped up against a shelf that was creaking under the weight of *Da Vinci Codes*. Overhearing one conversation between Martin and someone, I can count myself lucky as the former footballer explained that Pele had recently walked out of a signing session with hundreds of fans still waiting to meet him.

The queue finally ebbed away as the people of the little town of Bishop's Stortford exhausted their extended lunch hours. The one benefit of the waiting period was that my nerves got bored and left. I think watching the former Spurs director talking to so many people humanised him.

Finally I was waved over by the assistant. I'd been working on my opening line for so long that when I mumbled something about him having a sore wrist after all that signing, it could only sound crap. He took it well though and said it was all about the fans. Once he'd had a glass of water, we settled down to the nitty gritty.

My instructions were to get a straight news interview about his book and why he had come to the town. I swiftly eschewed that idea and started straight off by asking what he thought about England's first game. To my shock, he hadn't seen it as he'd been at a carnival where the big screens had failed. I quickly crossed out a load of questions about tactics and the heat problems with the game.

I asked about the squad and whether he was happy with it. As I had hoped, Martin – who still works at White Hart Lane on matchdays – was scathing in the exclusion of our boy Jermain. He saw no sense in taking two unfit strikers and then a youngster with no Premiership experience, when people like Defoe or even Darren Bent were ready and willing.

I then asked that, as he had come into the 1966 World Cup team in the second game of the tournament and remained a fixture from then on, could he see anyone else doing the same this year? He seemed a little cagey on this question, as if he'd been caught out before, and only answered that Sven didn't seem the type to tinker with his team.

I threw the name of Aaron Lennon at his grey-haired features and he merely shrugged and said he couldn't see anyone getting a chance.

Sensing he was more willing to talk about the past than the present, I hit the attacking midfielder with my killer question. Had he ever had a quiet moment where he wished that Wolfgang Weber had blasted his last-minute shot wide in the 1966 final rather than cancelling out his own half-volley 13 minutes from time? Would he have been comfortable being Sir Martin Peters – the man who won the World Cup for England?

With total modesty and a hint of annoyance, he swatted down the question as if it was a buzzing fly. "Of course not", he told me. It was all about the team and the glory for the country. With a slap on the wrist, I was informed that much of his book was taken up with praising the members of the squad who never got a chance to play in the finals. They may not have been seen by the crowds, but they were the ones who trained with the first eleven every day and were instrumental in capturing the trophy. It's a very charitable thought, even if I doubt it brings much solace to someone like Jimmy Greaves.

I asked if he'd struggled adjusting to life without football like so many of his contemporaries had. This seemed to get me back on his good side and he revealed that he did have a tough few years after retiring. He eventually started working for an insurance company and began to adjust. It seems mad that even a World Cup winner can be discarded as yesterday's news.

Slowly he got back into football in some sense and during Sir Alan Sugar's reign at White Hart Lane he was brought onto the board of directors. He took to the after-dinner speech circuit and now charges up to £7,000 a pop. After watching others bring out their autobiographies, he got together 18 months ago with a journalist from the *Evening Standard* to bring out his own version of events.

He spoke about recording *The Sun's* England anthem 'Who do you think you are kidding, Jürgen Klinsmann'. He had great fun with old West Ham and England team-mate Sir Geoff Hurst, but was rather distressed that in the latest charts, the ditty had been beaten by Stan Boardman and his chip shop bombing song.

Ode to Jol

Now 62, Martin Peters looks pretty much like a grey-haired version of the 22-year-old who shone at Wembley all those years ago. He's still slim and has retained the athletic poise of someone who drew England manager Alf Ramsey to say famously, "He's ten years ahead of his time".

I readied myself to ask about his thoughts on the current Spurs side, when his nameless aide came to whisk him away. The five minutes had disappeared faster than our Champions League chances. I shook hands with the legend and was left staring sadly at the unanswered questions sitting in my notebook.

Only days later and Tottenham's roadrunner got his chance to take on Martin's mantle. After 60 minutes of dull tripe against Trinidad and Tobago, Sven had a moment of excitement and threw Lennon and Wayne Rooney into the fray. Once again another player would provide the smokescreen for Lennon to get to work. Like Walcott's inclusion in the squad, Rooney's appearance drew our opponents' eyes away from the speedster on the right.

While it was a great sight to see Rooney back in action, he was simply feeling his way back into football. With Beckham moved to right-back, Lennon was given the freedom of the right and beat the left-back seconds after coming on. It was to turn into a trend and it wasn't long before one of his cut-backs was handled by Dwight Yorke, although calls for a penalty were turned away. The T and T defence were so concerned with the new width to the England side that they began to pull players out of the box.

Finally we capitalised when Lennon controlled a high ball from another substitute, Stewart Downing, and headed it down to Beckham who whipped it into the box. Peter Crouch grabbed himself a goal and a handful of Brett Sancho's dreadlocks. Lennon was again involved when he drew the left-back out before playing the ball again to Beckham who slipped in Steven Gerrard, who unleashed a wonderful strike into the goal from outside the box.

It took a few days for the hysteria over Rooney's appearance to dampen slightly and Lennon to receive some recognition.

I noticed Gerrard head over to the young winger at the final whistle, put his hand on his shoulder and congratulate him. In the press, Lampard and eventually Sven, after much prodding from the FA. have said how great he was with the Swede saying he is "knocking on the door" of the first eleven. Bloody answer the door then, Sven.

The pundits are split between using Lennon in a different formation, moving Beckham inside, and bringing Michael Carrick into the quarterback role behind Beckham, Gerrard and Frank Lampard. Both formations would probably mean losing Michael Owen. Do you substitute width for central power or strikers for midfielders? It's a difficult choice, but you can be sure that Owen Hargreaves will be involved in there somewhere.

The transfer gossip continues. Carrick was apparently certain to leave last weekend, but nothing seems to have happened on that front. It would be nice to hear something from the player himself, although England restrictions may mean he has to play and then get his own press conference for the question to be put to him. Rumours suggest that Spurs have banned all clubs from making approaches until after the World Cup and that they have their own bumper new contract lined up for his return. I'd rather he didn't leave as he's turned into a class individual, but we have the Hudd and the rather cracking looking Didier Zokora seems to be interested in joining us as well. Who knows what may happen?

The other floating rumours are that the Carlton Cole deal has been called off by us, we're still in for Damien Duff, we will pay £10m for Darren Bent, we're looking at Javier Saviola and finally Jermaine Jenas may quit Spurs as he is fed up with the positions he's being asked to play in.

Where do I start? I'm not too bothered about Cole unless he was purely a fourth striker, not a replacement for Defoe. If we signed Damien Duff I'd run around Tottenham with a Guinness top hat screaming "I love Ireland". I wouldn't want to lose legend in the making Defoe for either Saviola or Bent. However, if he demanded to leave due to his unhappiness, which doesn't seem to be the case in interviews or in MTV's *Goal* documentary series, then those two would be acceptable.

The Jenas story is the most ridiculous. With the emergence of Lennon, where else would he play except in the middle? He's stepped his career up a level at Spurs and has become a vital cog, winning over many of his doubters. When we lost his energy and running in the middle over the season, we didn't look as effective. Jol has turned him into the goalscoring midfielder he's always threatened to be. If he's unhappy then I'm wearing red right now.

Tuesday June 20th 2006

World Cup Group B
England 2 Sweden 2
Attendance – 45,000
England goalscorers – Cole, Gerrard

Wednesday June 21st 2006

I'M NOT SURE which better summed up my feelings towards England during this tournament – Michael Owen screaming in pain as a physio touched his ruptured cruciate ligament or Sven laughing like a hyena when Joe Cole scored his 35-yard scorcher.

Our campaign is swiftly turning into a farce. The Swede's ingenious plan to take Arsenal's kid for a holiday has blown up in his face like the entire world predicted. Our top goalscorer will play no further part in the tournament, Jermain Defoe is sitting at home sticking pins in a Sven doll and the 'clinical' Peter Crouch and a recovering Wayne Rooney are our only viable strikers.

You get the feeling that Eriksson would rather put David James up front than Theo Walcott. It would probably make more sense as at least Calamity has played a couple of minutes up front in the Premiership for Manchester City. That's more than Arsène's nephew. Even though he's a Gooner, I actually feel sorry for Walcott. He's just a kid mixed up in the middle of a pathetic publicity stunt that was meant to offset any loss of Wayne Rooney.

The sad thing is that Owen's loss could actually be turned into a positive by any normal manager. If Sven mysteriously went missing and Martin Jol was called in to take over for the remaining games, I'd envisage a midfield three of Beckham, Carrick and Gerrard with Cole and Lennon playing either side of Rooney. There's sexy football and then there's that formation.

Carrick would protect the attackers while he, Beckham and Gerrard spray the ball out to all corners of the pitch. The off-colour Lampard would be back-up on the bench. The triple threat up front would be terrifying to any defence. All three have pace, skills and end product. Chelsea use a similar system which can turn from defence into attack in seconds. If only.

Instead we will be stuck with a turgid, uninspired bland formation. He'll either shove Hargreaves in behind a midfield four, making us even more defensive and blunt than before. Fair play to Hargreaves, he put in an efficient first-half performance against Sweden with plenty of tackles. However, Carrick brings you that with the added bonus of pinpoint passing across the pitch rather than simple balls. The idea of a holding midfielder is to let Gerrard and Lampard get forward as they do for their clubs. Unfortunately, Hargreaves' simple passes mean at least one will always have to come back to collect the ball and you're back to square one.

The other thrilling formation is the tried and failed 4-4-2 snoozefest with Crouch up front. It's amazing what a tall striker can do to a talented team. Like Spurs and Mido, England's £100m midfield is bypassed because it's far easier to lump all those long balls onto Crouch's giraffe-like frame. There's no doubting Crouch bewilders opposition defenders, but his damage is better done as an impact sub as the performance against Argentina proved.

We should be able to beat Ecuador, but with Sven's tactics and predictable substitutions I can only see us struggling against quarter-finals opponents which could be either Portugal or Holland. Both sides have more attacking ambition than we can currently dream of. It's infuriating. The bespectacled one has inherited the best crop of English player sin decades. It's positively dripping with World Class status, yet he's managed to neuter it for the last five years. The midfield is the worst affected. Lampard and Gerrard are shadows of their club selves, while Beckham has been reduced to an American football-style kicker – only there to take the set-pieces

– and never to be removed from the field of play unless both his legs fall off.

To watch Eriksson guffawing after Cole's goal just proved he doesn't even expect quality to out. He was totally shocked by it all. It was similar to his overly dramatic exhaling of air after both England's late goals against Trinidad and Tobago. He's being paid £4.2m a year, so anything else is a bonus.

Enough of the doom and gloom. Heroes rise from troubled times and there's a little Lilywhite waiting on the bench to resume the beating he gave to T & T. Something may force Sven into using Aaron Lennon and then even the Swede won't be able to stifle the excitement and threat re-energising the team. Come on Azza, we're sending out an SOS – Save Our Summer.

Back at White Hart Lane, it's been quieter than Michael Carrick. Unlike his shy midfield partner, Jermaine Jenas came straight out and blasted reports of his unrest, saying he's never enjoyed football more than he is under the big Dutchman. The eternal reserve Johnnie Jackson and youngsters Claude Seanla and Marcel McKie have left to progress their careers in the lower leagues.

Damien Comolli is still apparently after the Ivory Coast's midfield general Didier Zokora, although we have competition from the Russian billions. Where Chelsea will squeeze him in I have no idea. Even at Spurs, if he's costing around £10m as reported, he'd surely only be coming if Carrick was on the way oop north.

However, it was good to see Martin Jol's statement this week that it "makes sense that we grow the squad, add quality players, keep our good players and give ourselves strength, depth and options." I hope that sense prevails, big man.

Sunday June 25th 2006

World Cup 2nd Round
England 1 Ecuador 0
Attendance – 52,000
England goalscorer – Beckham

ENGLAND STILL SEEM to be doing just enough to get by, so hopefully by that logic the players will up their game as the opposition improves.

Overall, it was a better performance today than in the previous matches. Michael Carrick was the difference. He put on a master class in the art of passing with both feet in front of the supposedly better Lampard, Gerrard and Beckham. Lifeguards were called into the BBC studio to save Gary Lineker and Alan Shearer from drowning in Alan Hansen's drool. They started to help Ian Wright, but decided to throw him back in.

With Michael sitting in front of the back four, England finally had that balance the side has craved for five years. Gerrard and Lampard at last had the freedom to get forward and do what they do week in, week out. Well that would have been the case had an impostor not slipped on a Lampard shirt and taken almost every shot around the Ecuadorian penalty area. They were flying into the crowd or worrying passing air traffic.

Had David Beckham not produced one of his awe-inspiring free kicks, I would certainly be screaming right now that Aaron Lennon is the round right peg for this round-holed formation. Saying that, you'd think the fact that the England captain threw up in the middle of the Stuttgart pitch shortly after his 60th-minute goal would have seen him withdrawn for the rocket-toed Lennon.

Don't be silly, this is Sven we're talking about. Instead he let a green-faced Beckham play on, looking completely exhausted and stooping with his hands on his hips for most of the time. Only three minutes from time did he bring on Azza. It was a mere cameo, but enough time to show what a clever head the kid has on such young shoulders.

He used his pace to optimum effect, running the defence ragged and taking a shot which could have resulted in a penalty as it hit the defender's hand. When a run was not on he took the ball into the corner and won throw after corner for England as the seconds and life drained away from Ecuador. Even Eriksson said he came on and did "very well". He's shown that the pressure and big match occasion doesn't mean anything – he'll always do what is required.

Mark "I can't believe I get paid to moan" Lawrenson decided that today's target of his bleating was Paul Robinson. The man who inspired Harry Enfield's 'Old Gits' got it into his head that it was Robbo's fault that John Terry had headed the ball into the path of the Ecuadorian striker Carlos Tenorio. Had England's Number One rushed out like Mr Charisma demanded then Tenorio would have rounded him and slotted the ball into an empty net.

As it was, Robbo jockeyed him into delaying his shot and Ashley Cole made up the ground and executed a perfect sliding block which deflected the ball onto the top of the crossbar. The only moment when Robinson did look shaky was when he came out to punch away a cross and ended up punching Rio Ferdinand's head. Who can be that angry with that, though? It pains me to agree with Ian Wright, but the only reason Robbo's mistakes are picked up is because he's normally so consistently class.

There was a scary moment when he went down clutching his knee. Suddenly the whole of next season flashed before my eyes. Although I think he may have felt a little twinge of pain, it could have been an elaborately hatched plan drawn up before the game to give the players a rest at a vital time in the second half. As soon as the physio ran across to him, the England players flooded to the touchline and poured liquids into their mouths and over their heads. It's surely no coincidence that a refreshed England controlled the game from then on.

At the opposite end of the pitch from our Robbo, Wayne Rooney was simply fantastic. I thought he looked knackered in the 90 degrees Fahrenheit heat during the first half, but he seemed to get stronger as the game went on. Unlike Owen, who still wasn't looking sharp after a couple of months back from injury, Rooney showed flashes in the second half of the rhinoceros-powered talent he is. He must have been exhausted, but he was skinning players with ease again and linked up well in the final minutes with Aaron Lennon.

It pains me in equal measure to say that both Ashley Cole and Sven's son Owen Hargreaves were excellent. Cole deserves that move to Real Madrid which has been in the offing for years and Hargreaves offered a lot more than the defensively minded Carragher. I'd still rather have Gary Neville there, though, if he recovers in time to play the more attacking-minded nations.

Talking of those, I've just watched the entertainingly crazy card-flooded game between Holland and Portugal. It made the England game look like a paint-drying contest. I was trying to decide which one I'd rather face in Saturday's quarter-final, but as it went on it became increasingly unclear which side would have enough players free to face us. In the end Portugal were the victors, but have lost Deco and Costinha to suspension. Cristiano Ronaldo limped off in the first half with a stud-imprinted thigh.

Lilywhites on the World Stage

To top that off Ricardo, Nuno Valente, Maniche, Figo and Petit will all be carrying yellow cards when they play us on Saturday. Surely, they will have a slightly more cautious approach than normal so as not to rule themselves out of a potential semi-final. It's going to be a cracker and time to avenge the defeat of two years ago. With Helder Postiga lurking on the bench, we should still be afraid... very afraid.

However, with another week to perfect the new formation and a step up in performance, I'd say we need not fear the European heavyweights. The extra man in the middle with Carrick will frustrate their passing style and Rooney will only get stronger. Gary Neville may be back and then there's that little guy on the bench – not the one holding Sven's hand.

The world of Tottenham Hotspur has been continuing on the home front as well as the world stage. Pictures came out this week on fan forums of Didier Zokora and Damien Comolli separately holding a Tottenham flag in the same German hotel bar with a young Spurs supporter. Then the *News of the World* carried quotes from the Ivorian midfield general saying that he had turned down Arsenal, Chelsea and Manchester United to seal an £8.5m deal with the North London giants.

Despite the club's usual reluctance to comment on speculation, they actually came out today to announce that they are in "advanced negotiations" with Zokora and his club, St Etienne. Having watched all his performances in the World Cup against the likes of Argentina and Holland, the man is a colossus with the energy of a cyborg. For anyone who may have missed him, think Edgar Davids crossed with Patrick Vieira.

Obviously his signing raises the old Carrick transfer saga again. With the amount of games Spurs will have to play this season, I would have thought he'd rotate with both Carrick and Jenas. Perhaps Jol has him in mind for a 4-3-3 with the three in midfield and Lennon and Keane/Defoe supporting Berbatov. That formation gives Defoe far more chances to play and impress as he can fill any of the attacking positions.

On Carrick, Chris Hughton was tracked down by Sky Sports today and said that it was not "inevitable" that the midfielder would leave and we'd already turned down two bids for him. He said we had no need to sell him, but the whole thing did smack a little of "we want to keep him, but it's up to him". As Carrick proved today, he's turning into a world-class player, but if he's going to hold us to ransom by saying he won't sign a new deal, then £15m will have almost paid for a goal machine and an Ivorian steamroller in his place. I'll shed a tear or two, but Carrick is not bigger than Tottenham Hotspur.

The new fixtures have been announced and we start our campaign away at the Reebok Stadium where the tumbleweeds blow. It's a tough opener, but it's about time we won there. The rest of the fixtures throw up one lovely fact. Unlike last year, we have no runs of top four side fixtures. They are nicely spread out, improving our chances of finally beating one of them no end. Rather than finishing the season away with illness at West Ham, next year will see us roaring on the side at White Hart Lane against Manchester City. Then we can all give them a standing ovation as they parade the Premiership trophy… well maybe.

Chapter Thirteen

July

Haven't we been here before?

Saturday July 1st 2006

World Cup Quarter-Final
England 0 Portugal 0 (1-3 on pens)
Attendance – 52,000
England penalty missers – Lampard, Gerrard,
Carragher

I COULD BE 10, 16, 18, 24 or 26 years old, because it's still the same outcome. A valiant, yet toothless, England performance ends in penalty heartaches and tears aplenty.

It's so depressing. Once again the player who was supposed to be the saviour ended up as the villain. Ironically, it was David Beckham who would comfort Wayne Rooney on the sidelines – the man who had seen a similar red mist eight years before. Whether Rooney was sent off for a push or a stamp is irrelevant. His nasty stamp on Ricardo Carvalho in the place cricketers quite rightly protect with a box deserved a red.

That sideshow around it will probably ensure Cristiano Ronaldo isn't the most welcome man at Manchester United's pre-season training ground return. You've got to be either the most patriotic or treacherous player to sprint over to a referee and try and get your own club team-mate sent off.

Ode to Jol

The BBC cameras picked up his little wink to the bench after the incident as if to say "Job done, lads". The cameras also captured him before the game smacking into Rooney's back and clearly saying something less than complimentary. Even the Scouse youngster looked surprised at the spotty winger's tactics. Ronaldo clashed with both Rooney and Gary Neville during the game and isn't the best of friends with Ruud Van Nistelrooy. Perhaps the claims that a Real Madrid presidential candidate will take him to Spain seem like a good idea.

What probably hurts the most about the whole experience is that we left our golden generation of world-class players in the hands of a bespectacled impostor with no imagination or balls. Player for player we had arguably the best squad in the tournament and that's including a small child who the Swede smuggled onto the plane to watch some matches for free. Just writing that makes my hands tremble with rage. Defoe should have been there instead of that Arsenal PR exercise.

At the end of the day, Sven played to accommodate his friends to the detriment of the team. We played with no verve or imagination and we were probably the poorest team alongside Ukraine to make the last eight. A newcomer to football would never know that the combined value of our team was north of £150m. It's so bloody disappointing.

The players can't all hide behind Sven's shadow. Lampard is supposedly the second best player in the world, yet he was among the worst players at the World Cup. Despite a couple of goals, Gerrard was nowhere near his usual self. They need only look at the central midfielders of supposedly lesser footballing nations like Ghana and the Ivory Coast for a lesson in world stage performances.

We created so few chances. I wonder how long

our typical battling British bulldog struggling against adversity performance will mask the total inadequacies of our play. I've just watched Sven asked whether his record of three quarter-finals was good enough for an England manager. He'd already said "sorry" 27 times in the early part of the interview, before saying that he would agree that the team was poorer in this tournament that the previous two.

For once we agree. I'd be tempted to say that was our worst World Cup showing in the last two decades. We went out earlier in 1998, but we never played with the lack of conviction and bluntness of this year. I certainly won't miss Sven and his strange ways. My only hope is that his ginger successor is not a chip off the Scandinavian block.

As Sven is full of apologies, I must offer mine to one player who has been on the receiving end of some harsh words in the last few weeks. Give me a slab of that humble pie, Mr Hargreaves, because today you were magnificent. While I would still suggest that Michael Carrick would have offered us more cutting edge in our attacks, the Bayern Munich man was everywhere.

I don't know what they feed them at the German club, but that guy was still sprinting around the pitch after two hours, while Gerrard and Lampard were wheezing with their hands on their hips. He was supposed to be our holding midfielder, yet he was playing like a box-to-box Duracell bunny. You may have kept out our boy Michael, but you proved you are a big-game player.

The only shining light for England in the whole tournament was the emergence of Aaron Lennon on the world stage. While any other manager would have accommodated the fastest man in Germany in their line-up, Sven would only use him as a side thought. It took a Beckham injury to finally get him some decent time on the pitch. Every time he touched the ball, something happened. With his immediately recognisable stiff-backed pre-sprint posture, he sparkled in front of the watching millions. He ghosted past players into the area to set up a misfiring, pre-red mist Rooney. He almost won a penalty and had he got more behind one shot that fell into Ricardo's hand, he could have covered himself in glory. Without him we looked bland. With him we had purpose and Portugal were never comfortable.

There's no point in even talking about penalty kicks, really. We even practised them this time, but it means not a jot. When an England player steps up for a penalty kick in a shoot-out, he has the weight of a nation, its media, its history and the spectre of Pizza Hut adverts on his shoulders. Until we come across a nation as pitiful at penalty shoot-outs as us, we'll never stand a chance.

We need a breath of fresh air through the squad. The old controlling heads need to pass on the baton to the next generation and our tactics and style need to advance to match the rest of the world. With our players we should be swaggering through games, not stumbling to hard-fought wins. Every tournament I moan about Spain and how they are the perennial under-achievers. I'm afraid my blinkered nature has deceived me. That title belongs to England.

Out of interest, I've heard there could be a big scandal breaking about Theo Walcott being sent home in disgrace before our game against Portugal. Apparently he failed a drugs test in front of FIFA officials, who found an unusually high concentration of Calpol in his system.

Joking apart, the weirdest thing of all is that my disappointment at that final kick was nowhere near the pain I felt on the final day of the season when an illness-ravaged Spurs side lost out on Champions League football. Despite my ranting and raving in pages past over Sven and his mess, the cockerel is stamped on my heart.

I have to use that 'tribal' word again, because I think that's where football fandom is heading. The more Spurs players in an England first eleven, the more interested I am. Am I alone in this? For me, the match today came alive when Aaron Lennon entered the fray.

Here's the killer question that may divide people reading this. Would you prefer Tottenham Hotspur win the Premiership or England win the World Cup? For me, it's the former every time. I'm all for national euphoria, but give me the choice and I'd take the personal satisfaction and pride of my club reaching the zenith. England is my side order, Spurs are my main meal.

Sunday July 2nd 2006

I WAS PLANNING to wait a day before commenting on Spurs matters over the last few days, but first I have to mention the two big fallout press conferences this morning.

David Beckham is no longer the England captain and he relinquished the armband today with tremendous dignity and emotion. While there were times in the last six years when his place in the team shouldn't have been so certain and his influence over players and selection always appeared to be too much, his passion was never in doubt.

Watching him give up his childhood dream with tears in his eyes was quite a sad experience. Whether he was pushed or just felt it was time for a new era, he was genuinely choked to quit. While he was more of a 'lead by example' captain than an inspiring, rallying one, there's no doubting he put everything into his role.

I have no problem with Beckham as a captain.

Especially in his younger, more energetic days, he drove the team forward. He hasn't quit international football and will make his 100 caps, but from now on right-midfielders like Aaron Lennon will have a chance to impress rather than watch and wish. I guess John Terry will be the favourite to take on the captaincy although Steven Gerrard can't be far behind. Both would do for me.

The other press conference was Sven's goodbye. It was telling that the reporters who have not let up on his inabilities over his reign barely put a testing question to him after our poorest tournament in years. Only Garth Crooks, an ex-footballer and ex-Spurs of course, put questions of any note to him.

The Swede was full of more apologies, but ultimately blamed the press for him leaving his role. Firstly, I would have been surprised if he hadn't been sacked after this World Cup anyway, despite Brian Barwick's bizarre claim that he has been a successful England manager. Secondly, the press have only reported on Sven's off-field scandals which have been of his own making and slaughtered his abysmal tactics and selection choices. Nobody forced you to commit any of your misdemeanours. You were just found out.

Eventually he was asked about the omission of Defoe, to which he gave his most stupefying answer yet. He told the media when asked whether he'd made a mistake: "I don't think so. If I had thought so I would have picked him. I've seen him 15 or 20 times this season and I have to take the best players, which I think will be good for us in the future."

Defoe's not good for the future? What has the Swede been smoking? Defoe certainly hasn't had a great season by his standards, what with all the chopping and changing up front at Spurs, but that doesn't change the fact that he's a class player. I don't quite understand how Eriksson can say Jermain can't play at this level when I seem to remember him being the one bailing the Swede out in qualifying against Poland on his first start. He was praising the backside off the boy then.

How dare he say that he has seen him "15 or 20 times" and deemed him not good enough? He's never seen Walcott play – even in his few Championship games – yet judged him to be good enough. However, when in Germany, he picked everybody available instead of the oblivious, iPod-listening youngster. I'm afraid our departing England manager contradicts himself at every turn. Goodbye, Sven, don't let the door hit you on the way out.

Enough about England anyway. That's done until the next penalty shoot-out exit. Damien Comolli has been a busy boy. A number of events happened as expected – Arsenal were cleared of wrongdoing by the FA and FIFA despite the BBC saying their evidence was overlooked, Stephen Kelly went to Birmingham and Didier Zokora finally signed this week.

The big man signed on a five-year deal and joined from St Etienne for an undisclosed fee, although reports estimated it to be around £8m. Martin Jol proclaimed that we had fought off a lot of other clubs to snap up one of the best midfielders in the World Cup and his performance certainly backed up that tag. It's been pleasing to notice on the internet that a lot of Gooners are concerned about his particular purchase, calling him the new Vieira.

The latest round of quotes from the Ivorian midfield general indicate that he actually met with Whinger before deciding that Tottenham's rebuilding plans were too appealing. He said that he wanted to take Spurs on to that next level they were striving for.

Ode to Jol

With Zokora's arrival comes an upsurge in the Carrick departure stories. The Goons and even Real Madrid have been linked with the midfielder Sven dumped like a bad Swedish meatball. The Spanish club's presidential candidate Lorenzo Sanz claimed that he has negotiated a deal with Carrick which will come into effect if he wins the election tonight. He's not the favourite though – that's Juan Miguel Villar Mir who has promised the signings of England's favourite stepover king Cristiano Ronaldo, Olympic diver Arjen Robben as well as Zico, Pele and some bloke called Ronnie Rosenthal.

If Carrick has to go – and there has still been no word from him – then I'd prefer it to be Madrid rather than another Premiership side. However, the figures being quoted now are nearer to £20m. With Zokora's signing then it would seem a tad mad not to accept that much money. It funds the purchase of both Didier and Dimitar Berbatov and leaves original funds for other players. That's two top-class players for one –seems a bit of a no-brainer.

Obviously, I'd rather he stayed and we were full to the brim with class at the Lane. He and Zokora could make a class partnership. It does mean we have 37 central midfielders and still no new faces for the left. I'm just going to go with what Martin Jol eventually decides. If Carrick wants to go then adios gringo – there are others, many many others.

I'm not particularly delighted by the club giving a new three-year deal to Anthony Gardner. While I admit that he ended up having a decent end of season, he won't break the King/Dawson partnership. He has a run of consistent, decent performances and then makes an amazingly bad mistake from a lack of concentration. He is also as comfortable on the ball as a legless performing seal. I think the Uefa Cup needs more quality in reserve.

Haven't we been here before?

West Brom confirmed we made a bid for Curtis Davies, which is on the right track. Surely we need someone of that stature and a young defender blooded and given a chance when injury permits. Dorian Dervette is coming along this month and Leigh Mills must be coming through the ranks soon, or will they be tossed out before being given a chance? If reports are true then Calum Davenport seems to be heading that way.

The new fan-dabby-dozy training ground application is still sitting with Enfield planning officers. Fans that live in the area are supporting it in their droves while a few other homeowners have objected to it all. The initial designs have been changed to incorporate concerns that cropped up during the consultation.

This means they have changed the design of the first team and academy centre, improved the layout of the training area and pleased the green types by using renewable energy and more efficient water use and recycling. The main local concern has been addressed by dropping proposals to build on the Bulls Cross Open Space.

The club will also launch a £2 million community programme for the borough of Enfield that should help the thousands of local schoolchildren. The plans certainly look impressive and it would upgrade our already impressive Spurs Lodge into one of the best training grounds in the world. Any visiting potential signing will never fail to be impressed. Rumour has it that most of Middlesbrough's big signings were swayed because of their training ground. Add the name Tottenham Hotspur to that equation and it can only equal success.

Elsewhere on the player front, Dean Marney has been linked with a move to Plymouth Argyle, which is quite likely as I can't see him getting past our army of central midfielders or those who can play on the right.

Ode to Jol

We've been linked with Marlon Harewood again which makes me shudder so much I don't want to talk about it anymore. There is also talk that Damien Duff is about to sign a new contract at Chelsea. That's a massive shame as he would have been superb at Spurs. Expect a new bid for Stewart Downing in the next few weeks.

There seems to be confirmation on other clubs' sites, but not our own, that we are playing friendlies this summer across Europe against Bordeaux, Nice, Celta Vigo and Borussia Dortmund. If those are confirmed by the club, then it's a clever plan. What could be better preparation for a Uefa Cup run than travelling across Europe playing the type of teams we will face? It's so much more professional than the old days of 38 friendlies against teams from the lower leagues, one Dutch side and Rangers or Celtic.

Talking of Europe, I've heard we'll be wearing a special chocolate brown kit for our continental campaign. If true, I'm sure there will be comparisons with a certain bodily waste product. However, the early signs are that it looks really smart and I think it would be a nice way to celebrate our return to European battle.

I can't wait until August 25th, when we will find out who we face in the Uefa Cup first round on September 14th. It's still unclear whether we will be seeded for the draw, but we shouldn't fear anybody. We are Super Tottenham from the Lane.

Chapter Fourteen
Final Thoughts

A YEAR HAS passed since I began this journal and the saga is finally drawing to a close at White Hart Lane. Star Wars may have taken 28 years to unfurl its full complement of tragedy, humour and thrills but the folks at Tottenham Hotspur have managed to squeeze as much action and drama into a single season.

Heroes have been born, villains have risen and some have fallen from grace and spectacularly turned to the dark side. Unfortunately Martin Jol has, as of yet, failed to challenge Frank Arnesen to a duel over boiling lava. I can just see him shouting: "You were the chosen one! You were meant to bring balance to the Lane!"

I honestly cannot think of a season I have enjoyed more while having frequent heart attacks. Sure, other campaigns have had glorious moments, such as the FA Cup win in 1991 after demolishing Arsenal in the semis, the League Cup win of 1999, or the arrival of the flying German, but none has been as consistently eventful and enjoyable as this one.

I'm a fully paid-up member of the cliché-ridden society which loves the rollercoaster metaphor. If that is to be applied to Spurs' 2005/06 season then one can only assume the ride was not fitted with brakes. The highs and lows have come at a thick and frenetic pace and, quite frankly, I still feel giddy with the adrenalin and my legs feel a little weak.

The campaign was all topped off typically with the farce that was the final day shenanigans. Never had a season so deserved to end with a triumphant victory. However, in typical Spurs style, drama had to come before joy. There was illness, accusations and inabilities. Daniel Levy slaved over a barnstormer of a letter, exposing all the deficiencies he saw in the Premier League and Richard Scudamore, who spent the final day linking arms with Gooners sending off the Library. Will he be cutting the ribbon on Cashburden Grove?

We never expected the West Ham game to be replayed. The tests were always going to come back with inconclusive results and the Premier League board was always going to sweep it under their reportedly red carpet. It was more important that we had the support of the majority of Premiership sides – we all know who would have opposed – and hopefully the rules will be scrutinised more closely in future. It's time to anaesthetise that slice of pain and remember what has been a truly brilliant season that will sit proudly among the pages of the club's history.

Spurs have probably spent more time on the back pages of the newspapers and in the media than any year in recent memory. The off-pitch antics of the season's opening and close have bookended some increasingly positive press for the North London club with our squad list beginning to resemble a who's who of England's stars present and future. I half expect Alan Hansen to wear a T-shirt next year on *Match of the Day* bearing the words "Tottenham Hotspur can win things with kids".

One man who should be getting a decent portion of the credit for this new era is surely the little guy at the top. A couple of years ago, Danny Boy took flak from all sides for sacking Glenn Hoddle, then leaving the maestro Pleat in charge while taking what seemed an age to appoint a new manager. Then when he finally put a new system in place to ensure the stability of the club's future, he was attacked by the media for changing the good old British way. Many journalists did all they could to snipe at the changes and tug at the seams. The little guy just couldn't win.

Things got worse when, only months in, Santini left. However, much to the shock of the media, the structure held and Jol was promoted from within. The new arrangement began to bear fruit as the Spurs youngsters built up some serious momentum and started to make a real European push. Strangely it took the poaching of our dastardly Sporting Director to make the hacks finally admit that a pretty decent set of changes had taken place in N17.

When Arnesen left with roubles in his eyes, there was no wallowing in the tragedy of it all from Levy, just a single-minded mission to get compensation for a heinous act of treachery and skulduggery. Sir Alan Sugar has been getting a lot of post-Spurs praise searching for an Apprentice, but his successor at the Lane is well on his way to achieving cult status for reinventing the ailing club.

Whatever bad luck struck on the last day, the successes have far outweighed the disappointments this year. Jol has transformed things on the hallowed turf and his work on the training ground is clear for all to see. A host of players have stepped up to the plate and delivered. Robinson, King, Keane, Carrick, Davids, Lennon, Dawson, Jenas, Tainio and at times, Mido, have made their mark in the Premiership and some at international level with style and bravado.

Massive forward steps have been made on the pitch and off. Yes, we had enough chances to get into the Champions League, but ultimately fell short. However, the experience gained by playing through the pressure of this campaign and then next year's Uefa Cup will be invaluable to the progression of our youngsters. The new breed of Lilywhites have once again brought a fluid passing style to the green green grass of Tottenham and a smile to fans young and old.

How many times in previous years have I wailed at the screen as another scrappy move fell apart and resulted in a goal for the other side? Nowadays the style and swagger has returned to White Hart Lane and the place has become a fortress once more. Teams don't expect to come along and win; in fact most brace themselves for an onslaught of pressure and shots as Mr Opta and his stats rightly prove.

The fact that we actually had an exciting season run-in for the first time in three centuries is testament to the big man in the Spurs crested blazer. When, in recent years, have we been cheering our team on with such ferocity on the final day of the season? It was a very unusual feeling but an extremely welcome one. I loved every minute of it even if I was practically in tears by the end of May 7th.

Even the drama of Darth Arnesen's treachery had unexpected silver linings. The flying Dutchman moved to centre stage and continually proves that he can motivate thousands of people with a mere sentence. Rarely a day goes by when the Jolly Orange Giant doesn't come out with a classic quote.

I'll always remember "Maybe he doesn't realise how strong I am", about Arsène Wenger's touchline hysteria, and "Maybe on Saturday hundreds of squirrels will come on to the pitch and we will have a problem. You cannot prepare yourself for squirrels, so we would probably have to run." The man is a comic legend. Think Eddie Izzard with a growl.

The furore and disappointment of the Premiership season's close will only serve to make the club and us

252

fans wiser and stronger. The more they try to beat us down the more it proves that we're heading in the right direction. If people are trying to steal our players or staff, it's simply because they are jealous or they want to stop us overtaking them.

The tide is certainly turning in North London. The French Foreign Legion has never been as bothered about us or spoken as much about us in years. We outplayed them for the majority of both our meetings this season and they know it. The only thing that kept them above us this season was a dodgy meal and a self-adoring world-class striker. They're running scared and their elation and relief on the final day is a testament to the strides Big Martin has made with the side.

I'd never seen Wenger squeal in a high-pitched voice about "Tottingham zis" and "Spurs zat" before this campaign. Next season they will have to face us and they will come across a dominating team with experience of a long and pressurised season. The old, ageing Spurs has been reinvigorated with a Dutch flavour and even suspect food won't keep us down next time. Apparently David Pleat is being brought back into the fold as a meal tester.

The foundations are in place, the talent is growing every day and we're heading on an exciting European adventure next season. After a summer of recharging batteries and refreshing our zeal, it'll be time to dust off the passports. We were the first club to lift the Uefa Cup in 1971 and 35 years on we will return to the competition stronger than ever.

Gone are years of dreaming. Everyone on the board, coaching and playing staff is finally pulling in the same direction and the club is beginning to deliver on its promise to give us our Tottenham Hotspur back. I can feel the hairs rising on my arms as the European glow on the horizon offers the chance to witness a new chapter in Tottenham history.

We have had to suffer enough false dawns, bogus messiahs and treacherous turncoats in such a short space of time that it's about time we enjoyed the kind of golden age our predecessors have waxed lyrical about. There's a big man at the helm with even bigger talent and the ability to inspire all those around him. He was brought to Spurs with far less fanfare than his higher profile colleagues, but has eclipsed them with ease as their disloyalty came to the fore.

It was somewhat fitting that in 2004, when Bill Nicholson, the greatest manager in Tottenham Hotspur's long and proud history, passed away, the man who could one day prove to be his heir emerged from within his beloved club.

The times are changing, the revolution is almost complete and a dozing old club is waking up with a new saviour leading it to the Promised Land. Our cockerel is going to be crowing loudly across the continent next season. I hope you will join me for the adventure. This has been my Ode to Jol.

Other football books from SportsBooks

Wembley – The Complete Record 1923–2000
Every football match ever played at the world's most iconic football stadium is detailed in this exhaustive reference work. Paperback. ISBN 1899807 42 X £14.99

Ha'Way/Howay the Lads
A history of the rivalry between Newcastle United and Sunderland. Paperback. ISBN 1899807 39 X £14.99

Accrington Stanley - the club that wouldn't die
Accrington Stanley returned to the Football League this year after resigning in 1962. This tells the story of the years of struggle and eventual triumph. Hardback. ISBN 1899807 47 0 £16.99

Black Lions - a history of black players in English football
The story of black players in English football, with interviews with players such as Garth Crooks, John Barnes and Luther Blissett. Hardback. ISBN 1899807 38 1 £16.99

Harry Potts – Margaret's Story
Harry Potts was Burnley's manager in the days the small-town team won the league and reached the FA Cup final. This is his story told by his widow Margaret and Dave Thomas. Great photographic section. Hardback. ISBN 1899807 41 1 £17.99

Fitba Gallimaufry

Everything you wanted to know about Scottish football and a lot of things you didn't want to know as well. Hardback. ISBN 1899807 45 4 £9.99

Growing up with Subbuteo – my dad invented the world's greatest football game

Mark Adolph tells the story of growing up with his father Peter, the man who invented Subbuteo. A very funny, often poignant account of life with an eccentric father. Hardback. ISBN 1899807 38 1 £16.99

Europe United – a history of the European Cup/Champions League

The story of the European Cup/Champions League. Hardback. ISBN 1899807 30 6 £17.99

Raich Carter – the biography

The only man to win an FA Cup winners medal before and after the war and the man England preferred to partner Stanley Matthews. Hardback. ISBN 1899807 18 7 £16.99

The Complete Centre-Foward – a biography of Tommy Lawton

The only man to win an FA Cup winners medal before and after the war and the man England preferred to partner Stanley Matthews. Hardback. ISBN 1899807 09 8 £14.99